LOOKING FORWARD

Molly von Heider

Activities to develop
children's learning abilities.

Games, rhymes and exercises for children aged
three – eleven years of age.

Gardening with Young Children

Hugh Peters

HAWTHORN PRESS

Published by Hawthorn Press, 1 Lansdown Lane, Stroud GL5 1BJ, U.K.

Looking Forward Copyright © 1995 M.W. von Heider
Gardening with Young Children © 1995 Hugh Peters

Cover design by Patrick Roe
Typeset in Plantin by Saxon Graphics Ltd, Derby
Printed and bound in Great Britain

A catalogue recording this book is available from the British Library
ISBN 1 869 890 67 1

Childhood

I see all, am all, all.
I leap along the line of the horizon hill,
I am a cloud in the high sky,
I trace the veins of intricate fern.
In the dark ivy wall the wren's world
Soft to bird breast nest of round eggs is mine,
Mine in the rowan-tree the blackbird's thought
Inviolate in leaves ensphered.
I am bird-world, leaf-life, I am wasp-world hung
Under low berry-branch of hidden thorn,
Friable paper-world humming with hate,
Moss-thought, rain-thought, stone still thought on the hill.
Never, never, never will I go home to be a child.

By Kathleen Raine, from
Selected Poems 1935 – 1980,
Harper Collins Publishers Limited

Contents

Introduction

This book is designed to help teachers find the kind of movement which will benefit the children in their early years, and lay the foundation for a sound learning process.

Teachers should not resort to Eurythmy, which is a new art of movement and requires specialist teachers who have had 4–5 years' training.

A thread of wisdom runs through the old singing games and verses. Today, through the educational works of Rudolf Steiner, we are able to look back and read the hidden, unconscious motive toward a healthy development in these old 'nonsense' verses and street games. We are not just going back to the past but bringing an understanding which can enable us to create new kinds of movement out of traditional games.

What are the child's needs in the different stages of development? In the days before radio, television, computers and audio-visual technology, it was possible for the child to develop certain cognitive abilities partly through play.

Today most schools need therapists and certain hospitals have paediatric departments where therapists work with so-called ineducable children; many of their exercises echo the 'old' games. By the time that intellectual disabilities in writing, reading, spelling or maths are recognised, it may be too late in the child's school life to remedy them effectually.

Teachers can learn to become 'prophylacticians' by looking ahead and knowing what difficulties could be in store for the child, difficulties which could often be avoided by practising the right kind of movement at the right time.

In Steiner Schools children work together within their own age group. They are not divided into classes according to their ability.

Class	Age
I	6 + 7
II	7 + 8
III	8 + 9
IV	9 + 10
V	10 + 11

Acknowledgements

I would like to express my gratitude to Kathleen Raine for permission to include "Childhood" as an introduction to *Looking Forward*. (From Kathleen Raine, *Selected Poems 1935 – 1980*, Harper Collins, London).

My thanks also go to the 1992 Emerson College Education students for their persistent demands for games and activities for the lower school, and especially to Helen Bawden of Ringwood Rudolf Steiner School for triggering off the actual writing of this book two years ago in Norway.

I am most grateful to Roy Wilkinson for his guidance and to Rosemary Gebert for her sound advice. Also to Fiona von Heider for her good counsel, especially concerning gardening and the environment, and for her insistence on consistency.

I am much indebted to Hugh Peters for permission to use his treatise on gardening, and to the late Sophie Poulson of Norway for the cover of this book. A special thank you to Roswitha Spence and Kristin Ramsden for the drawings and to Jonathan Godber for the Speech Exercises, and to Kate Hammond for her patience in typing and retyping this book.

My sincere apologies to the authors of the *Grammar Verses* and "*The Waves and the Ship*", whose names I have been unable to find.

Learning Aids

The following indications when interwoven with the teaching will strengthen the child's formative forces, ie. the ability to learn.

1. All movement that takes the child off the ground, skipping, jumping, climbing, balancing, dancing (not Classical)
2. Eurythmy
3. Skilful feet and fingers
4. Working with anticipation
5. Rhythm, repetition (forwards and in reverse)
6. Experiencing the Language of form
7. Engaging the child whole-heartedly
8. Memory training
9. Order out of chaos

In the early years of childhood teachers should be aware of the benefit to children of working consciously with the senses, especially the four will senses.

The sense of Touch:	Experiencing boundaries; also developing sensitivity of the hands and fingers.
The sense of Life:	Experiencing the feeling of well-being. Free play.
The sense of Movement:	Self-movement.
The sense of Balance:	Orientation.*

*See the *Twelve Senses* by A. Soesman, Hawthorn Press, 1990 or John Davy, *On Coming to Our Senses*, in *Hope, Evolution & Change*, Hawthorn Press, 1983.

A Bibliography for the above indications, is included after the Conclusion page.

The Early Years

During the first seven years the child learns by imitation. The child learns to speak by imitation. But, today many children cannot imitate. How can we develop this important faculty? In experiments carried out in Russia it was observed in most cases that non-imitators had either stiff red fingers and toes or soft 'doughy' fingers or toes. Warmth and massage of the hands and feet resulted in a growing ability to imitate sounds and thus gradually learning to speak.[1] Dr Steiner stresses that the child must become an ardent imitator if he is ever to be a free human being.[2] We cannot begin too early warming and enlivening children's hands and feet and playing finger and toe games with them.

Finger games can continue during the first seven or eight years of a child's life not only in English but also from the child's 5th year in foreign languages. The more dexterous the child is with fingers and feet the better the cognitive centre in the brain develops and thus the child's ability to learn is strengthened.

Feet

It is of utmost importance in these early years to foster the flexibility of the child's feet.

The arch of the foot begins to form at about the age of five. This can be helped by encouraging the children to pick things up with their feet such as marbles, handkerchiefs, little sticks, also daisies on the lawn. Try walking on the toes, on the heels, on the outside and on the inside of the feet – also drawing and writing with the feet. All these exercises can be carried out in an imaginative way so that they bring fun and laughter.

Flatfootedness inhibits a good upright posture and can cause backache and headaches when the child is older.

Nylon socks, nylon shoe lining, synthetic or ill-fitting shoes tend to prevent healthy growth and mobility of the feet and thus the child's

[1]   Prof. Dr Med M Kolzowa, Leningrad, Kind Tanzt, Dr H von Kügelgen.
[2]   Rudolf Steiner, *Education as a Social Problem*, Lecture 1, Dornach, 9–17 August 1919.

learning ability could also be affected. The feet tell us eloquently about the child's state. Teachers need to 'read' their message and 'see' them as well as the childrens' shining faces.

If necessary, advise parents of the care needed for the feet if children are to go through school without too many health and learning difficulties.

Foot Exercises
Kindergarten or Class I,
5–7 Years

There was an old cobbler
and he lived by himself,
   But
He had a little helper
And he was an elf
All day long they would sing this song
And cobble magic shoes to fit everyone.

Hammering Rip, rap, tick, tack,
   Tick-a-tack-a-two.
   Scarlet leather sewn together
   This will make a shoe,
   Left, right pull it tight
   Summer days are warm,
   Underground in winter
   Laughing at the storm.

   Walk on outside of feet
There came a poor farmer with funny feet,
with funny feet, with funny feet
There came a poor farmer with funny feet
And he could never, never find any shoes to fit.
   Puts on magic shoes
Now I can jump and I can spring
I can skip and dance in a ring
hurrah, hurrah, hurrah.
   Tip toes
There came a tiny tailor with funny feet
with funny feet, with funny feet
There came a tiny tailor with funny feet

And he could never never find shoes to fit.
   On heels
There came a burly baker ...
   Inside
There came a chimney sweeper ...

Finger Games

A woodpecker pecked out a little round hole
  Peck at the closed hand with thumb and forefinger until a 'hole' appears
And made him a nest in a telephone pole
One day when we watched he poked out his head
  Push thumb and forefinger through the 'hole'.
He had on a hood and a collar of red.

When the rain comes down from the dark grey sky
  Both hands imitate falling rain and lightning
and the flashes of lighting go zig zagging by
and the big wheels of thunder roll *stamp with both feet*
He snuggles down into his little round hole... *as lines 3 and 4*

✦ ✦ ✦

Here is the beehive
but where are the bees?
  Hidden away where nobody sees.

Here they come creeping   *Out comes the thumb and then the*
  Out of the hive   *fingers of one hand, through the*
One, two, three, four, five   *other hand which remains half-*
  buzz, buzz, buzz   *closed as the beehive.*

✦ ✦ ✦

The Riders of the rain
At night I heard a ratatattat   *Children tap with their*
Twas not a drum beat was true.   *fingers on the floor.*
I listened long and then I knew
It was the riders of the rain.

But with the rising of the dawn
There was no sound of any hooves
The riders of the rain had gone
To ride on other children's roofs.

✦ ✦ ✦

Here is father hare
   Close one hand then stretch up forefinger and middle finger as ears.
Here is mother hare   *Repeat with other hand.*
Where are all the baby hares?
Here they come hopping   *Both hands 'hop' around.*
Hippity hop, hippity hop over the ground
And they can cross their ears
   Cross fore- and middle fingers of both hands.
Without making a sound.
   From Finland

Open them, close them
Open them, close them
  Give a little clap
  Lay them in your lap
Creep them, creep them down to your knee
Creep them, creep them up to your chin
Open your little mouth, but don't put them in.
Open them, close them, give a little clap *above the head*
And lay them in your lap.

✦ ✦ ✦

I found a little cherry stone
   Pretend to pick up a stone.
And put it in the ground
   Partly close the other hand and put the 'stone' in the hollow.
Next time when went to look
A tiny shoot I found.
   Push forefinger slowly through partly closed hand.

The shoot grew upward day by day   *Whole hand and wrist appear*
And soon became a tree   *Stretch fingers*
And now I pick the cherries off   *Pluck at finger tips*
And eat them for my tea.

Where is Thumbkin?

Where is Thumb-Kin? Where is Thumb-Kin? Here I am! Here I am! "How are you to-day, sir?"

"Very well I thank you." Run a-way Run a-way

Where is Thumbkin? Where is Thumbkin?
Here I am! Here I am!
"How are you today, sir?"
"Very well I thank you."
Run away
Run away

Repeat with: Pointer or Foreman, Taliman or Middleman, Ringman, Littleman or Pinky, The Whole Family

The Birds' Nest

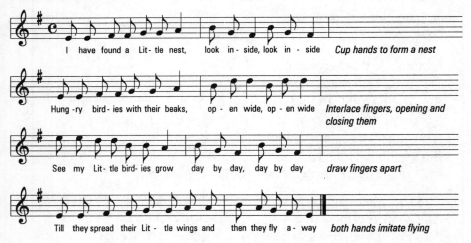

I have found a Lit-tle nest,   look in-side, look in-side   *Cup hands to form a nest*

Hung-ry bird-ies with their beaks,   op-en wide, op-en wide   *Interlace fingers, opening and closing them*

See my Lit-tle bird-ies grow   day by day, day by day   *draw fingers apart*

Till they spread their Lit-tle wings and   then they fly a-way   *both hands imitate flying*

I have found a Little nest, look inside, look inside
Hungry birdies with their beaks, open wide, open wide
See my Little birdies grow day by day, day by day
Till they spread their Little wings and then they fly away

Five Little Ducks

Five little ducks went swimming one day
Over the pond and far away
Mother duck said "Quack, quack, quack"
and four little ducks came swimming back

Last verse: One little duck ...
Father duck said, "Quack, quack, quack"
and five little ducks came swimming back.

The fingers of one hand are the ducks, the other hand is mother duck quacking with thumb against the 4 close stretched fingers

My Pigeon House

My pigeon house I open wide and I set all my pigeons free.
They fly around on ev'ry side and perch on the highest tree.
And when they return from their merry flight, they close their eyes and say Goodnight.
'Coo-oo Coo, Coo-oo Coo, Coo-oo Coo, Coo-oo Coo, Coo-oo Coo, Coo-oo Coo Coo-oo.'

Close hands together then open them and let fingers 'flutter' away and back. Close hands together

Dance, Thumbkin, Dance

Dance, Thumbkin, Dance!
Dance, Thumbkin, Dance
Thumbkin cannot dance alone,
so dance, ye merry men, ev'ry one
And dance, Thumbkin, dance!

Repeat with other fingers

The Eency, Weency Spider

The Eency Weency Spider crawled up the water spout.
Down came the rain and washed the spider out.
Out came the sun and dried up all the rain.
And the Eency Weency spider crawled up the spout again.

Right thumb and index finger climb on left index finger and thumb

Looking Ahead

Much has been written about the historic or ritualistic origin of the singing games which have been handed down through the centuries. Many of these games, enjoyed by the child, do not make ready sense to the adult. What is their value in education today?

If we look collectively, take an overall view, we find that singing games, street games, tell us the story of life from birth to death. This motif is to be found in every country; there are Dutch, French, German, Scandinavian, African, Maori and American versions and so on and variations of English themes.

Does playing and dancing the 'story of life' in the 'dream time' of childhood endow us with those forces needed to face later life more consciously?

The following are examples of qualities that can be engendered through play.

Imitation

We need to be ardent imitators[3]

There are many games in which we learn to imitate, not only household tasks but also the skills of craftsmen. Although washing machines, vacuum cleaners, mechanical devices and farm machinery have now taken over, the traditional manual movements, are for the most part, performed with joy and vigour by the children.

The games can be played at different ages; some are more suitable for the pre-school and kindergarten child. Other games such as *The Miller* and *Knots of May*, are for the eight year old children.

Awareness of Self and the World

This ninth year experience of being outside, of standing alone and facing the world, could be called *Leaving Home*. This is expressed in the following singing games:

[3] Rudolf Steiner, *Education as a Social Problem*, Lecture 1, Dornach, August 1919.

Sally go round the sun
Green gravel
Water, water wall flower
Round and round the village
Knots of May
There was a jolly miller

MARRIAGE   ***The Farmer in the dell***
            Poor Jenny
DEATH   ***Old Roger is dead***

Sally go round the Sun

Sally go round the sun
Sally go round the moon
Sally go round the chimney pot on a Saturday afternoon.
Whoopy!

The children circle round. On chimney-pot each child makes his/her own little circle. On whoopy all take hands and go to the centre.

Green gravel

Green gravel, green gravel, your grass is so green
The fairest young maiden that ever was seen.
We washed her, we dried her we clothed her in silk
and we wrote down her name with a gold pen and ink.
O Mary* O Mary your true love is dead,
And we send you a letter to turn round your head.

Green gravel, green gravel, your grass is so green
The fairest young maidens that ever were seen.
We washed them, we dried them we clothed them in silk
and wrote down their names with a gold pen and ink etc.
O maidens O maidens your true loves are dead,
And we've sent you some letters to turn round your heads.

*Child's name.

The chosen one turns and faces outward. This is repeated until all have turned

Water, Water, Wallflower

Water, water wallflower growing up so high
We are all God's children and we all must die,
except for the fairest of us all,
She can dance and she can sing and she can do the Highland fling
Fie, fie, fie for shame. Turn your face to the wall again.

The children join hands and dance round in a ring. At 'except for' a child's name is given. At 'fie for shame', the children stand still and wave a forefinger at the child named who turns and faces outwards, but is still part of the circle. The game continues until all the children are facing outwards. Then the song is sung once more and last line is, "Turn your face to the ring again".

Variation. Instead of singing one child's name, a group of children can be chosen by singing "except for those wearing blue", next time "wearing red" and so on.

Irish Version.
Wall flowers, wall flowers growing up so high
We all get the measles but never, never die
Go to 'Mary's' house he/she has no relations
     'Peter's'
He/she can kick and cack and turn his/her back and kiss the congregation.

Round the Village

1). Round and round the vil - lage, Round and round the vil - lage, Round and round the

vil - lage, As we have done be - fore.

1. Round and round the village,
Round and round the village,
Round and round the village,
As we have done before.

2. In and out the windows, etc.
3. Stand and face your partner.
4. Follow him/her to London.
5. Jumping over the doorstep.
6. Shake hands before you leave him/her.

Those in the circle kneel down and join hands, the pair jump over and go to the centre of the ring.

Knots of May

1). Here we come gath - er - ing Knots of May, Knots of May, Knots of May. Here we come gath - er - ing
2). Who will you have for your Knots of May, Knots of May, etc.
3). We'll have _____ our Knots of May, Knots of May, etc.

Knots of May, On a fine and sum- mer morn - ing.

Here we come gathering Knots of May,
Knots of May, Knots of May.
Here we come gathering Knots of May,
On a fine and summer morning.

Who will you have for your Knots of May, Knots of May, etc.

We'll have _____ our Knots of May, Knots of May, etc.

2nd 4. Who will you send to fetch her away
1st 5. We'll send _____ to fetch her away
All 6. At twelve o'clock the battle begins.

Players form two equal lines facing one another. Each line as it sings, advances towards the other and retires. The two named try to pull one another over a handkerchief or other mark. The one who is pulled over is the 'captured knot' and joins the other side. Then the song is repeated, the second side beginning verse 1.

In and out the Bonnie Bluebells

In and out the bon - nie blue - bells, In and out the bon - nie blue - bells, In and out the
bon - nie blue - bells, You shall be my part - ner! Pit - ta pat - ta pit - ta pat - ta
on your shoul - ders, Pit - ta pat - ta pit - ta pat - ta on your shoul - ders
pit - ta pat - ta pit - ta pat - ta on your shoul - ders, You shall be my part - ner.

In and out the bonnie bluebells,
In and out the bonnie bluebells,
In and out the bonnie bluebells,
You shall be my partner!
Pitta patta pitta patta on your shoulders,
Pitta patta pitta patta on your shoulders,
Pitta patta pitta patta on your shoulders,
You shall be my partner.

The children stand in a circle holding their arms up to make arches. The leader moves in and out of the arches and stops behind a child, the 'partner'. The leader taps on the child's shoulders and the child follows. Next round two do the tapping and then the four and so on until the last children have joined the chain and it becomes a ring again.

The Jolly Miller

8-9 years

English Traditional

There was a jol-ly Mil-ler and he sat by him-self as the wheel went round he made his wealth with one hand on the hop-per and the oth-er on his bag, as the wheel went round he made his grab.

There was a jolly Miller and he sat by himself
as the wheel went round he made his wealth
with one hand on the hopper and the other on his bag,
as the wheel went round he made his grab.

Couples are formed and march round in a ring singing, one circle to the right, the other to the left. The Miller is in the centre. At the word 'grab' everyone links arms with someone going in the opposite direction. The Miller also tries to get a partner. The one who is left out becomes the Miller.

Poor Jenny a-weeping

1.) Poor Jen - ny sits a - weeping, a - weep - ing, a - weep - ing, poor
3.) I'm weep - ing for a part - ner, a part - ner, a part - ner, I'm

Jen - ny sits a - weep - ing, on a bright sum - mer's day.
weep - ing for a part - ner on a bright sum - mer's day.

2.) Pray Jen - ny tell me what you're weeping for, a - weeping for, a - weeping for, pray

D.C. vs. 3, 4

tell me what you're weep - ing for, on a bright sum - mer's day?

4.) Pray, get up and choose one etc.

Now you're married we wish you joy, first a girl and then a boy:

seven years af - ter, son and daugh - ter, Pray young couple come

dance to - geth - er. Dance round once, dance round twice, dance round three times o - ver.

Poor Jenny sits a-weeping, a-weeping,
a-weeping,
poor Jenny sits a-weeping, on a bright
summer's day.

Pray Jenny tell me what you're weeping for,
a-weeping for, a-weeping for,
pray tell me what you're weeping for,
on a bright summer's day?

I'm weeping for a partner, a partner, a partner,
I'm weeping for a partner on a bright summer's
day.

Pray, get up and choose one etc.

Now you're married we wish you joy,
first a girl and then a boy:
seven years after, son and daughter,
Pray young couple come dance together.

Dance round once, dance round twice,
dance round three times over.

Old Roger is Dead

Old Roger is dead and laid in his grave,
Laid in his grave, laid in his grave
Old Roger is dead and laid in his grave,
Heigh-ho! laid in his grave.

2. They planted an apple tree over his head, etc.
3. The apples grew ripe and they all fell off, etc.

4. There was an old woman came picking them up, etc.
5. Old Roger got up and gave her a knock, etc.
6. That made her go off with a skip and a hop, etc.

Oats and Beans and Barley Grow

Oats and beans and barley grow,
Oats and beans and barley grow,
but not you nor I nor anyone knows
how oats and beans and barley grow.

First the farmer sows his seed,
then he stands and takes his ease
stamps his feet and claps his hands
and turns him round to view the land.

Waiting for a partner (twice)
Open the ring and let one in
And take her (him) to the centre.

Now you're married you must obey
you must be true to all you say,
you must be kind, you must be good
And help your wife to chop the wood.

The Farmer in the Dell

The farmer's in his dell.
The farmer's in his dell.
Heigh-ho the derry-O,
the farmer's in his dell.

2. The farmer wants a wife, etc.
3. The wife wants a child, etc.

4. The child wants a nurse, etc.
5. The nurse wants a dog, etc.
6. The dog wants a cat, etc.
7. The cat wants a mouse, etc.
8. The mouse wants a cheese, etc.
9. The cheese stands alone.

On a Monday Morning

Poland

On a Monday morning,
Sunny Monday morning,
Sowed the Wheat, Tartuffe and I,
sowed it when the sun was high,
Sowed the wheat, Tartuffe and I,
sowed it when the sun was high.

Tuesday ... cut the wheat
Wednesday ... gathered the sheaves
Thursday ... threshed the wheat
Friday ... ground the grain
Saturday ... baked the bread
Sunday ... ate the bread.

'Tartuffe' Polish for 'Father' pronounced
'Tattoosh'

The Mulberry Bush

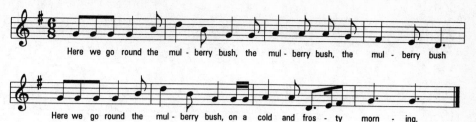

Here we go round the mulberry bush, the mulberry bush, the mulberry bush
Here we go round the mulberry bush, on a cold and frosty morning.

2. This is the way we wash our clothes, etc.
3. This is the way we iron our clothes, etc.
4. This is the way we scrub the floor, etc.

Or one can stress actions like:
Brush our hair
Clean our teeth
Wash our hands

Who'll Come Into My Wee Ring?

A Scots game for the tinies.

Who'll come into my wee ring,
My wee ring,
My wee ring?
Who'll come into my wee ring,
And make it a wee bit bigger.

2. I'll come into your wee ring
   And make it a wee bit bigger.

Adam He Had Seven Sons

Adam he had seven sons,
Seven sons had he.
They would not eat, they would not drink,
but they all went just like me.

Follow My Leader

Follow my leader to London town,
London town, London town;
Follow my leader to London town,
So early in the morning.

2. Sadly and slowly to London Town,

3. Running along to London Town,
4. Stamping along to London Town,
5. Hopping along to London Town,
6. Skipping along to London Town,
7. Walking quietly to London Town.

I Went to Kindergarten

From Finland

I went to Kindergarten and I walked like this,
walked like this, walked like this,
I went to Kindergarten and I walked like this,
All on my way to school.

I saw a little robin and he hopped like this, etc.

I saw a shiny river and it splashed like this, etc.
I saw a little pony and he galloped like this, etc.
I saw a tall policeman and he stood like this, etc.
I heard the teacher calling and I ran like this, etc.
And when I got to school I sat quietly like this, etc.

3½ years

The young child lives in the 'dream-time'

5½ years

After five the child begins to find his feet and awaken to the world

Classes I and II – Ages 6, 7 and 8

The child's school life usually begins between the ages of 6 and 7.[4] The awakening and releasing of the intellectual or formative forces begins slowly around the child's sixth year. It is the time when the child draws pictures of houses, pictures of rainbows, pictures of the sky high above, and the earth and a little house and flowers and people far below, pictures which illustrate inner awareness of a separation from the heavens and leaving the child's oneness with the world to live in his own little 'house' and become an individual.

In many educational lectures Rudolf Steiner describes how between the ages of 6 and 7 the child changes and renews his model body, his first teeth come out and new ones push through – growth forces[5] loosen and in part become intellectual forces.[6] The child is now ready to learn to write, read and do arithmetic.

Should this freeing of certain life forces[7] for intellectual work not take place, should the child quite unconsciously not want to grow up, then disturbances, weakness in the harmonious development of the formative forces manifest themselves as dyslexia, kleptomania and in some cases, hyperactivity or autism.

How can we help the birth of the intellect through movement at this crucial time?

All movement that takes the child off the ground helps to release the life forces – so skipping, hopping, jumping, climbing, dancing are all healthy activities for the 6 and 7 year olds.

In the past children skipped to school, skipped in the playground, chanted skipping rhymes. Children introduced skilful variations and speeds into the art of skipping. They skipped alone, in pairs, in groups,

[4] Rudolf Steiner, *Human Values in Education*, Lectures II, IV and VIII, Arnhem, 17–24 July 1924.
[5] Rudolf Steiner, *A Modern Art & Education (Ilkley Course)*, Lecture IV 5–17 August 1923.
[6] Intellectual forces, growth forces, life forces, formative forces – characterized by Rudolf Steiner as etheric forces.
[7] As above.

counting and chanting as they skipped, even skipping Double Dutch as two ropes turned.

Skipping is a wonderful co-ordination exercise. Teachers of 6, 7 and 8 year old children could introduce it when the children are learning numbers and counting.

Skipping Games

Divide the class in half: one half 'the counters' the other the 'skippers'. The teacher and a tall child rotate the rope towards the line of 'skippers' who run under the rope, at first one child at a time, then two children together, then three, and so on, while the 'counters' count 1, 2, 3 etc; 2,4,6 etc; and 3, 6, 9 etc.

Variations
The rope can be wriggled sideways like a snake for a long jump or turned into waves for a higher jump. The children can also skip one at a time, then two together, then three while the 'counters' count and the 'skippers' skip.

Some good skipping rope games are not suitable for the classroom, but can be played out of doors. The teacher only needs to go out and start a craze, a game such as 'The Fisherman'. Here the teacher stands in the middle of a circle swinging a rope with a bean bag tied on one end. The children jump when the bean bag, describing a circle, nears them. If the bean bag touches one of the children the fisherman has caught a fish and the child is out. The children learn to anticipate the speed of the rope and judge when to jump.

In our age of video games, played alone, children are not so likely to begin to play games together and they may need the class teacher to start them off.

Skipping Rhymes

Cups and saucers   *swing the rope below*
Plates and dishes
Little brown men
In scarlet breeches   *then count the skips*

Andy Pandy   *swing the rope over the head of the*
Sugary candy   *crouching child*
French almond ROCK   *jump up and skip*
Salt, mustard, vinegar
PEPPER   *very fast*   England

Bread and butter for your supper
Is all your mother's got
The high skip, the sly skip
The low skip, the tow skip
They skip altogether,
They skip double double,
The fast skip, the last skip
They skip against trouble

Bluebells, cockle-shells,
Eevy, ivy, over.
My mother sent me to the store,
And this is what she sent me for:
Salt, vinegar, mustard, pepper,
Salt, vinegar, mustard, pepper...   Canada

Apples, peaches, pears, and plums,
Tell me when your birthday comes.
January, February, March...   Canada

Two people stand and turn the rope. They and all the waiting 'skippers' chant:

All together boys,
This fine weather boys,
When's your birthday boys?
Please jump in!
      January, February.....December   England

The child jumping jumps the months of the year. If no mistake is made then the whole sequence is repeated faster and faster.

Variations
The child jumping must only come in when his birthday month has been reached and he skips out again when it comes round again.

Group Variation
Children join in as and when their birthday month is reached, they go through the cycle and out again.

Third Variation
As originally, the whole sequence plus second sequence very fast and if the child is still not out, then the rhyme is repeated with the words 'please jump *out*'.

Ball Bouncing

Throwing and catching are also necessary experiences at this time. They are breathing, expansion and contraction exercises. Bean bags are best for throwing in counting games in the classroom, they lie where they fall and do not roll about under desks, but the times-tables can be learnt while bouncing a ball.

Ball Bouncing   Devonshire

1) Ordinary juggling of balls against a wall. Right hand throws from under.

One, two, three and plainsy
four, five, six and plainsy
seven, eight, nine and plainsy
ten and plainsy carry on!

2) One, two, three and overs	On word 'over' the right hand throws one over
3) 1, 2, 3, 4 dropsy	Ball must rebound off wall and bounce on floor once before being caught again
4) 1, 2, 3, 4 and double dropsy	Ball must bounce twice on floor
5) 1, 2, 3, 4 and smalk'em	Ball is thrown on the floor and must be bounced up onto the wall and off again and then be caught
6) 1, 2, 3, 4 and unders	Under left leg
7) 1, 2, 3, 4 and spinsy	Spin full circle on 'spinsy' in time to catch ball again
8) 1, 2, 3, 4 and knock 'em	Run, back to wall and bounce ball between legs so it hits floor then rebounds onto wall and back to you

Ball Bouncing   America

Tennis size ball, bouncing on the ground

One, two, three O'Leary
four, five, six O'Leary

Ten O'Leary post catch.
First right leg out and over the ball
Second left leg out and over the ball
Third right leg in
Fourth left leg in
Fifth hold skirt and make a hoop for the ball to go through
First over then under
Should a mistake occur, the sequence must begin again.

There are very many health-bringing exercises, games and plays we can do in Class I and II if we bear in mind the numerous indications Rudolf Steiner has given for the strengthening of the learning forces, the formative or etheric forces in his lectures on Education.

If we continue now with the exercises that 'take the child off the ground', the old folk dance 'A-Hunting We Will Go' is a splendid example. The slip step must be performed so that the child's feet really clap together, the higher and lighter the children can jump, the better. If the words displease, another rhyme can be created but the music and dance form are just right for this age group. The slip step can also be used as a gallop. At the end of a story the children can dance together in twos round the circle singing 'they all lived happily ever after, ever after, ever after, they all lived happily ever after'.

A-Hunting We Will Go

A-hunting we will go,
A-hunting we will go,
Hey-ho the derry-O,
A-hunting we will go.

Original Verse
A-hunting we will go,
A-hunting we will go,
We'll catch a fox and put him in a bos
And never let him go.

The dancers stand in two lines, each has a partner opposite.
The top pair take hands and slip-step down and up the centre
then they skip down outside their row and make an arch, the
others follow and skip up the centre. The second couple is now first couple.
Slip step: a leaping side step.

The eurythmy exercise known as 'I,A,O' (EE, AH, OH) was given originally for uncoordinated children. It should be left to eurythmists to
practise with these children and should not be done by class teachers.
Exercises for bending and stretching and contraction and expansion
and stepping can be done with the whole class instead.[8]

I can curl up small
as round as a ball
I can be

I can stretch up tall
as straight
as a tree

✦ ✦ ✦

I can walk, walk, walk
I can hop, hop, hop
I can dance, dance, dance
I can skip, skip, skip
    and
I can stop, stop, stop.

✦ ✦ ✦

The foxes move so softly you cannot hear a sound
The trotting ponies' hoofbeats are thudding on the ground
And all Class I in breaktime go skipping merrily round.

✦ ✦ ✦

The earth is firm beneath my feet,
And upright I can stand.
The heavens arch above my head,
My friends are here on either hand.

Games, stories and images that have been handed down to us from
generation to generation often appear simple. If we can learn to 'read'

[8] Rudolf Steiner *Curative Eurythmy Course*, Lecture 1 (last 2 pages), Dornach, 12–18
April 1921 and Stuttgart, 28th October 1922.
Dr. Kirchner-Bockholt M.D., *Fundamental Principles of Curative Eurythmy*, Chapter 5,
Rudolf Steiner Press.

this legacy we can find great wisdom. It can be for us like a sign post pointing the way ahead out of the past. The motifs behind the games and images can assist the class teacher in the early years to strengthen the formative forces in order to prepare the child for intellectual work.

Many children today are neither right handed nor left handed. This impedes their ability to learn to write, read and do arithmetic. One side should be strengthened, preferably the right side.

Playing tops, whipping and whipping the top with the right hand (or left) again and again, helps to develop the child's cognitive centre. Hoop bowling was a similar activity which is no longer possible on our car-ridden roads. Hopscotch, five stones, stilts, marbles, conkers and cats' cradles are all therapeutic games which usually began naturally according to the season.

Working with Anticipation

This can be introduced quite simply by the way we speak to the children. For instance, instead of saying 'Who would like to be the prince today?' say, 'Now I am going to choose someone to be the prince'. Then instead of chaos and a chorus of 'me, me, me', there will be quiet in the classroom and each child will be reaching out inwardly toward being the prince. Of course each child must have his turn eventually. Also tell the children at the close of the day what lessons they will be having tomorrow and who will be the helpers to water the plants, prepare the paints, and so on.

There are games where this element of anticipation is prevalent: all counting out games, skipping, ball throwing and ball bouncing, writing a letter or drawing a simple picture on the child's back. Two children together, one drawing and the other one guessing. Then change over if the guess was correct.

This is especially good for excarnated children. Also *Cobbler, Cobbler, mend my shoe.* Here is another gym or playground game:

All the children stand in a group, except one child who stands a little way in front with his back to the group and throws a ball over his head; whoever catches it hides it behind his back, the thrower turns and has to guess who has the ball. The ball can be passed on to the other children secretly. If the thrower guesses correctly he has another turn, if not the child with the ball becomes 'the thrower'.

For the Class II children a birthday game called 'Creakers' was invented. A track was set up, a painting board balanced between two desks under which the birthday child must crawl, three rows of jam-jars (usually used for water in painting lessons), were placed across the path and must be stepped over without being knocked, two desks to climb over and so on round the classroom to reach the birthday card or present. All this must be performed in absolute silence. Should a board creak, the birthday child could choose a friend to complete the course and bring the present to him or her. There was silence in the classroom, the children held their breath; the game demands care and skill – clever feet and fingers make for good learning ability. Such games are not a waste of time, the children settle down quickly and quietly and are more attentive afterwards, BUT teachers must know what they are trying to achieve and why such games are beneficial for this age group.

Rhythm – Repetition

This does not mean classical rhythm in music or poetry such as the anapest u u -[9]. Children should dance and march to their 'own' rhythms and not be made too conscious of 'set' rhythms before the ninth year. If they can step or dance a rhythm naturally, all is well but they should not be made to do it consciously.

Care should be taken with stamping and clapping. Some children get quite out of themselves with loud clapping and stamping. It is better to 'hammer' with one closed hand against an open hand, than clap in these early years.

In ancient times the priests and leaders knew how to strengthen the life forces of their peoples through repetition. We see this in such Epics as the Kalavala, the Passover Chant,[10] the Sayings of Buddha. Many folk tales and poems echo this motif of rhythmical repetition.

Verses	*The Key of the Kingdom*
	The Tree in the Wood or The Rattling Bog
	The House That Jack Built
	The Twelve Days of Christmas
Stories	*The Little Pancake*
	The Turnip
	The Cock and the Hen in the Hazel Wood
	The Old Woman and the Pig
	The Boy who wouldn't go to school

Such poems and stories train the child's memory. This is important in Classes I, II and III.

All number counting should always be done forwards and backwards, at first with stepping or skipping or throwing beanbags. Also the tables, the days of the week, the months of the year, this too strengthens the child's learning ability.

[9] Rudolf Steiner, *Art in the Light of Mystery Wisdom.* "The Human Being's Experience of Tone", Lecture II, March 8th 1923.
[10] Rudolf Steiner, *The Gospel of St Mark*, Lecture IV, Basel, 15–24th September 1912.

The following two examples are included to show how in ancient times, the element of repetition was a necessary part of human development and was used by the priests and those with wisdom to strengthen their people. These two examples are not intended to be taught to the children: they are part of a ritual.

One only kid, one only kid, which my father bought for two zuzim; one only kid, one only kid.

And a cat came and devoured the kid, which my father bought for two zuzim; one only kid, one only kid.

And a dog came and bit the cat, which had devoured the kid, which my father bought for two zuzim; one only kid, one only kid.

Then a staff came and smote the dog, which had bitten the cat which had devoured the kid...

Then a fire came and burnt the staff which had smitten the dog...

Then water came and extinguished the fire which had burnt the staff...

Then the ox came and drank the water which had extinguished the fire...

Then the slaughterer came and slaughtered the ox, which had drunk the water...

Then the angel of death came and slew the slaughterer who had slaughtered the ox...

Then came the Most Holy, blessed be He, and slew the angel of death who had slain the slaughterer, who had slaughtered the ox, which had drunk the water, which had extinguished the fire, which had burnt the staff, which had smitten the dog, which had bitten the cat, which had devoured the kid, which my father bought for two zuzim; one only kid, one only kid.

This parable is regarded as descriptive of incidents in the history of the Jewish nation, with some reference to prophecies yet unfulfilled.

From the Book of the Passover

Who knoweth one? I, saith Israel, know one: One is the Eternal, who is above heaven and earth.

Who knoweth two? I, saith Israel, know two: There are two tablets of the covenant — but One is the Eternal who is above heaven and earth.

Who knoweth three? I, saith Israel, know three: There are three patriarchs, the two tablets of the covenant – but One is the Eternal who is above heaven and earth.

Who knoweth thirteen? I, saith Israel, know thirteen: There are thirteen divine attributes, twelve tribes, eleven stars, ten commandments, nine months preceding childbirth, eight days preceding circumcision, seven days in the week, six books of Misnah, five books of the law, four matrons, three patriarchs, two tablets of the covenant – but One is the Eternal who is above heaven and earth.

Green grow the Rushes-O

I'll sing you one-oh
Green grow the rushes-oh!
What is your one-oh?
One is one and all alone
And evermore shall be so.

I'll sing you two-oh
Green grow the rushes-oh!
What is your two-oh?
Two, two the lily-white Babes[11]
Clothed all in green-oh
One is one and all alone
And evermore shall be so.

I'll sing you three-oh
Green grow the rushes-oh!
What is your three-oh?
Three are the strangers at your door,
Two, two the lily-white Babes
Clothed all in green-oh
One is one and all alone
And evermore shall be so.

[11] In some versions, Lilywhite Boys
Three, three are Rivals
Five the symbols at your door
or
Six for the echoing waters

I'll sing you four-oh
Green grow the rushes-oh!
What is your four-oh?
Four are the Gospel Maidens
Three are the strangers at your door,
Two, two the lily-white Babes
Clothed all in green-oh
One is one and all alone
And evermore shall be so.

I'll sing you five-oh
Green grow the rushes-oh!
What is your five-oh?
Five is the Ferryman in his boat,
Four are the Gospel Maidens
Three are the strangers at your door,
Two, two the lily-white Babes
Clothed all in green-oh
One is one and all alone
And evermore shall be so.

I'll sing you six-oh
Green grow the rushes-oh!
What is your six-oh?
Six is the cheerful Waiter,
Five is the Ferryman in his boat,
Four are the Gospel Maidens
Three are the strangers at your door,
Two, two the lily-white Babes
Clothed all in green-oh
One is one and all alone
And evermore shall be so.

I'll sing you seven-oh
Green grow the rushes-oh!
What is your seven-oh?
Seven are the seven Stars in the sky,
Six is the cheerful Waiter,
Five is the Ferryman in his boat,
Four are the Gospel Maidens

Three are the strangers at your door,
Two, two the lily-white Babes
Clothed all in green-oh
One is one and all alone
And evermore shall be so.

I'll sing you eight-oh
Green grow the rushes-oh!
What is your eight-oh?
Eight are the eight Archangels,
Seven are the seven Stars in the sky,
Six is the cheerful Waiter,
Five is the Ferryman in his boat,
Four are the Gospel Maidens
Three are the strangers at your door,
Two, two the lily-white Babes
Clothed all in green-oh
One is one and all alone
And evermore shall be so.

I'll sing you nine-oh
Green grow the rushes-oh!
What is your nine-oh?
Nine is the Moonshine bright and clear,
Eight are the eight Archangels,
Seven are the seven Stars in the sky,
Six is the cheerful Waiter,
Five is the Ferryman in his boat,
Four are the Gospel Maidens
Three are the strangers at your door,
Two, two the lily-white Babes
Clothed all in green-oh
One is one and all alone
And evermore shall be so.

I'll sing you ten-oh
Green grow the rushes-oh!
What is your ten-oh?
Ten are the Ten Commandments,
Nine is the Moonshine bright and clear,

Eight are the eight Archangels,
Seven are the seven Stars in the sky,
Six is the cheerful Waiter,
Five is the Ferryman in his boat,
Four are the Gospel Maidens
Three are the strangers at your door,
Two, two the lily-white Babes
Clothed all in green-oh
One is one and all alone
And evermore shall be so.

I'll sing you eleven-oh
Green grow the rushes-oh!
What is your eleven-oh?
Eleven are the Eleven who went to Heaven,
Ten are the Ten Commandments,
Nine is the Moonshine bright and clear,
Eight are the eight Archangels,
Seven are the seven Stars in the sky,
Six is the cheerful Waiter,
Five is the Ferryman in his boat,
Four are the Gospel Maidens
Three are the strangers at your door,
Two, two the lily-white Babes
Clothed all in green-oh
One is one and all alone
And evermore shall be so.

I'll sing you twelve-oh
Green grow the rushes-oh!
What is your twelve-oh?
Twelve for the Twelve Apostles,
Eleven for the Eleven who went to Heaven,
Ten for the Ten Commandments,
Nine for the Moonshine bright and clear,
Eight for the eight Archangels,
Seven are the seven Stars in the sky,
Six is the cheerful Waiter,
Five is the Ferryman in his boat,

Four are the Gospel Maidens
Three are the strangers at your door,
Two, two the lily-white Babes
Clothed all in green-oh
One is one and all alone
And evermore shall be so.

The Story of the Boy who wouldn't go to School

Once upon a time there was a boy who would not go to school. His old mother went to the birch rod and said, 'Birch, birch, whip the boy, he won't go to school'.

But the birch rod would not.

So she went to the fire and said, 'Fire, fire, burn birch, birch won't whip boy and the boy won't go to school.'

But the fire would not.

So she went to the water and said, 'Water, water quench fire, fire won't burn birch, birch won't whip boy and the boy won't go to school'.

But the water would not.

So she went to the ox and said, 'Ox, ox, drink water, water won't quench fire, fire won't burn birch, birch won't whip boy and the boy won't go to school.'

But the ox would not.

So she went to the butcher and said, 'Butcher, butcher, slaughter ox, ox won't drink water, water won't quench fire, fire won't burn birch, birch won't whip boy and the boy won't go to school.'

But the butcher would not.

So she went to the rope and said, 'Rope, rope hang butcher, butcher won't slaughter ox, ox won't drink water, water won't quench fire, fire won't burn birch, birch won't whip boy and the boy won't go to school.'

But the rope would not.

So she went to the rat and said, 'Rat, rat, gnaw rope, rope won't hang butcher, butcher won't slaughter ox, ox won't drink water, water won't quench fire, fire won't burn birch, birch won't whip boy and the boy won't go to school.'

But the rat would not.

So she went to the cat and said, 'Cat, cat, eat rat, rat won't gnaw rope, rope won't hang butcher, butcher won't slaughter ox, ox won't drink water, water won't quench fire, fire won't burn birch, birch won't whip boy and the boy won't go to school.'

But the cat would not.

So she said to the cat, 'Cat, cat I'll give you a saucer of cream.' Then the cat ate the rat, the rat gnawed the rope, the rope hung the butcher, the butcher slaughtered the ox, the ox drank the water, the water quenched the fire, the fire burnt the birch, the birch whipped the boy and then .... off went the boy to school.

Translated from the Swedish by Malin Ask.

The Cock and the Hen in the Hazelwood

Once upon a time the cock and the hen went into the hazelwood to gather nuts.

The hen got a nutshell stuck in her throat and she lay there flapping her wings. The cock ran off to fetch water for her. When he came to the spring he said, 'Dear spring, please give me water for Hickety, my dear hen who is fighting for her life in the hazelwood.'

The Spring answered, 'You'll get no water till you bring me some leaves.'

So the cock ran off to the Linden Tree and said, 'Dear Linden Tree, please give me leaves for the Spring, who will give me water for Hickety, my dear hen who is fighting for her life in the hazelwood.'

The Linden Tree answered, 'You'll get no leaves till you bring me ribbons of red gold.'

So the cock ran off to the Virgin Mary and said, 'Dear Virgin Mary, please give me ribbons of red gold to give to the Linden Tree, who will give me leaves for the Spring, who will give me water for Hickety, my dear hen who is fighting for her life in the hazelwood.'

The Virgin Mary answered, 'You will get no ribbons from me until you bring me two shoes from the Shoemaker.'

So the cock ran off to the Shoemaker and said, 'Dear Shoemaker, please give me two shoes for the Virgin Mary, who will give me ribbons of red gold to give to the Linden Tree, who will give me leaves for the Spring, who will give me water for Hickety, my dear hen who is fighting for her life in the hazelwood.'

The Shoemaker answered, 'You will get no shoes from me until you bring me bristles from the Sow.'

So the cock ran off to the Sow and said, 'Dear Sow, please give me bristles for the Shoemaker, who will give me two shoes for the Virgin Mary, who will give me ribbons of red gold to give to the Linden Tree, who will give me leaves for the Spring, who will give me water for Hickety, my dear hen who is fighting for her life in the hazelwood.'

The Sow answered, 'You will get no bristles from me until you bring me corn from the Farmer.'

So the Cock ran to the Farmer and said, 'Dear Farmer, please give me corn for the sow, who will give me bristles for the Shoemaker, who will give me two shoes for the Virgin Mary, who will give me ribbons of red gold to give to the Linden Tree, who will give me leaves for the Spring, who will give me water for Hickety, my dear hen who is fighting for her life in the hazelwood.'

The Farmer answered, 'You'll get no corn from me until you bring me a bannock from the Baker.'

So the cock ran off to the Baker and said, 'Dear Baker, please give me a bannock for the Farmer, who will give me corn for the sow, who will give me bristles for the Shoemaker, who will give me two shoes for the Virgin Mary, who will give me ribbons of red gold to give to the Linden Tree, who will give me leaves for the Spring, who will give me water for Hickety, my dear hen who is fighting for her life in the hazelwood.'

The Baker answered, 'You'll get no bannock from me unless you bring me some wood from the Woodcutter'.

So the cock ran to the Woodcutter and said, 'Dear Woodcutter, please give me some wood for the Baker, who will give me a bannock for the Farmer, who will give me corn for the Sow, who will give me bristles for the Shoemaker, who will give me two shoes for the Virgin Mary, who will give me ribbons of red gold to give to the Linden Tree, who will give me leaves for the Spring, who will give me water for Hickety, my dear hen who is fighting for her life in the hazelwood.'

The Woodcutter answered, 'You'll get no wood from me unless you bring me an axe from the Smith.'

So the cock ran to the Smith and said, 'Dear Smith, please give me an axe for the Woodcutter, who will give me some wood for the Baker, who will give me a bannock for the Farmer, who will give me corn for the Sow, who will give me bristles for the Shoemaker, who will give me two shoes for the Virgin Mary, who will give me ribbons of red gold to give to the Linden Tree, who will give me leaves for the Spring, who will give me water for Hickety, my dear hen who is fighting for her life in the hazelwood.'

The Smith answered, 'You'll get no axe from me unless you bring me charcoal from the Charcoal Burner.'

So the cock ran to the Charcoal Burner and said, 'Dear Charcoal Burner, please give me charcoal for the Smith, who will give me an axe for the Woodcutter, who will give me some Wood for the Baker, who will give me a bannock for the Farmer, who will give me corn for the Sow, who will give me bristles for the Shoemaker, who will give me two shoes for the Virgin Mary, who will give me ribbons of red gold to give to the Linden Tree, who will give me leaves for the Spring, who will give me water for Hickety, my dear hen who is fighting for her life in the hazelwood.'

The Charcoal Burner felt sorry for the cock and gave him charcoal.

So the Smith got charcoal, and the Woodcutter an axe, and the Baker the Wood and the Farmer a bannock and the Virgin Mary two shoes, and the Linden Tree ribbons of red gold, and the Spring the Linden leaves and the cock water for Hickety, his dear hen, who drank and no longer had to fight for her life in the Hazelwood.

from Norway

This is the Key

This is the key of the kingdom:
In that kingdom is a city;
In that city is a town;
In that town there is a street;
In that street there winds a lane;
In that lane there is a yard;
In that yard there is a house;
In that house there waits a room;
In that room an empty bed;
And on that bed a basket –
   of flowers, of flowers;
   A basket of sweet flowers.
Flowers in a basket;
Basket on the bed;
Bed in the chamber;
Chamber in the house;
House in the weedy yard;
Yard in the winding lane;
Lane in the broad street;
Street in the high town;
Town in the city;
City in the kingdom –
This is the key of the kingdom.
   Of the kingdom this is the key.

Traditional

The Rattlin' Bog

With zest   Traditional Irish

O ro the ratt-lin' bog, bog down in the valley - O

O ro the ratt-lin' bog, bog down in the valley - O

1.) And in this bog there grew a tree, a rare tree, a rat-lin' tree,

tree in the bog and the tree in the bog and the (etc....)
branch on the tree and the

bog down in the valley - O

O ro the rattlin' bog, bog down in the valley-O
O ro the rattlin' bog, bog down in the valley-O

1. And in this bog there grew a tree, a rare tree, a rattlin' tree,
tree in the bog and the tree in the bog and the (etc...)
bog down in the valley-O

2. And on this tree there was a branch...
3. And on this branch there was a twig...
4. And on this twig there grew a leaf...
5. And on this leaf there was a nest...
6. And in this nest there was an egg...
7. And on this egg there sat a bird...
8. And from this bird there came a feather...
9. And from this feather there came a pillow...
10. And on this pillow there slept a boy...

The Twelve Days of Christmas

A Forfeit Game

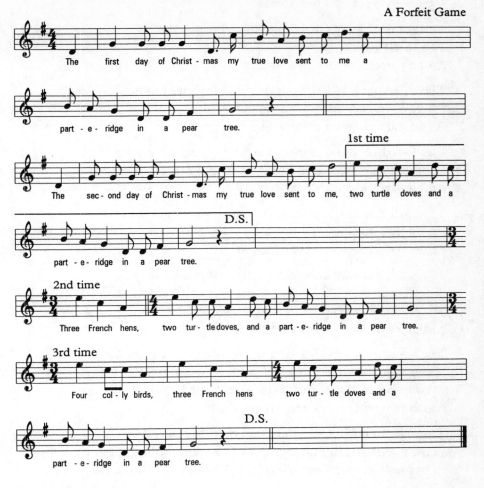

The first day of Christ-mas my true love sent to me a part-e-ridge in a pear tree.

The sec-ond day of Christ-mas my true love sent to me, two turtle doves and a part-e-ridge in a pear tree.

1st time

D.S.

2nd time Three French hens, two tur-tle doves, and a part-e-ridge in a pear tree.

3rd time Four col-ly birds, three French hens two tur-tle doves and a part-e-ridge in a pear tree.

D.S.

A colly bird is a thrush

The first day of Christmas, my true love sent to me
A part-e-ridge* in a pear-tree.

The second day of Christmas, my true love sent to me
Two turtle doves,
And a parteridge in a pear-tree.

The third day of Christmas, my true love sent to me
Three French hens, two turtle doves,
And a parteridge in a pear-tree.

The fourth day of Christmas, my true love sent to me
Four colly-birds,† three French hens, two turtle doves,
And a parteridge in a pear-tree.

The fifth day of Christmas, my true love sent to me
Five gold rings, four colly-birds, three French hens, two turtle doves,
And a parteridge in a pear-tree.

The sixth day of Christmas, my true love sent to me
Six geese a-laying, five gold rings, four colly-birds, three French hens,
  two turtle doves,
And a parteridge in a pear-tree.

The seventh day of Christmas, my true love sent to me
Seven swans a-swimming, six geese a-laying, five gold rings, four
  colly-birds, three French hens, two turtle doves,
And a parteridge in a pear-tree.

The eighth day of Christmas, my true love sent to me
Eight maids a-milking, seven swans a-swimming, six geese a-laying,
  five gold rings, four colly-birds, three French hens, two turtle
  doves,
And a parteridge in a pear-tree.

The ninth day of Christmas, my true love sent to me
Nine drummers drumming, eight maids a-milking, seven swans a-
  swimming, six geese a-laying, five gold rings, four colly-birds,
  three French hens, two turtle doves,
And a parteridge in a pear-tree.

* This is not the usual spelling but it is correct for this carol.

The tenth day of Christmas, my true love sent to me
Ten pipers piping, nine drummers drumming, eight maids a-milking,
    seven swans a-swimming, six geese a-laying, five gold rings, four
    colly-birds, three French hens, two turtle doves,
And a parteridge in a pear-tree.

The eleventh day of Christmas, my true love sent to me
Eleven ladies dancing, ten pipers piping, nine drummers drumming,
    eight maids a-milking, seven swans a-swimming, six geese a-laying,
    five gold rings, four colly-birds, three French hens, two turtle
    doves,
And a parteridge in a pear-tree.

The twelfth day of Christmas, my true love sent to me
Twelve lords a-leaping, eleven ladies dancing, ten pipers piping, nine
    drummers drumming, eight maids a-milking, seven swans a-
    swimming, six geese a-laying, five gold rings, four colly-birds,
    three French hens, two turtle doves,
And a parteridge in a pear-tree.

An old Christmas game, played especially on Twelfth Night. The party
sit round the room. The Leader says the first verse, each repeats it in
turn. Then the leader says the second verse, which each repeats. And so
on. For every mistake a forfeit is given up. At the end, the forfeits are all
cried, and redeemed.

The Language of Form

One of the most important subjects in these early years is form drawing. It is not only an aid to writing but a unique tool for developing the child's 'growing up' process in a healthy way.

Between the ages of seven and fourteen the child has certain abilities which die away later. These abilities, these forces can be strengthened and exercised through form drawing when the child enters school.[12]

What is this form drawing? How can we as teachers experience and prepare ourselves to teach this new subject?

We can begin by opening our eyes to the living forms in the plant kingdom. We can also look back to the architectural forms of the past. What do we experience standing under a Gothic Arch? In a crypt, in a choir? Why did the Celts, the Greeks, the Maoris and the African peoples so love the spiral? Why are the patterns on African pottery akin to those found on the pillars of European churches? Why did the people of the Northern Lands develop the intricate ribbon patterns that are carved on the Viking boats, chariot, sledges and weapons also painted in the Book of Kells and other Missals and enamelled on early English jewellery?

Some patterns contain the essence of folk legends. The crossing of the Pacific to the Land of the Long White Cloud (New Zealand) by the Polynesians is depicted in spiralling waves. The climb to the heavens in search of food, in the simple step pattern so often found in Maori weaving and the curves depicting the heaven (Rangi) and the earth (Papa).

Did not the Greeks in the Doric, Ionic and Corinthian Columns with the Palm and Pomegranate motif, the ramshorn spirals and the Acanthus also with its spirals, bring the same catharsis as the fear and compassion evoked in their tragedies? Do not these forms bring about a rhythmical healthy breathing?

[12] Rudolf Steiner, *Practical Advice to Teachers*, Lecture 1, Stuttgart, 21st August–5th September 1919.

This is the canoe crossing the waves between
Hawaii and New Zealand.

'Poutama' ~ Steps to Heaven

The Druids experienced the Celtic Sun Cross saying, 'The sun has come
to dwell on earth.'

The insignia on Rudolf Steiner's Mystery Plays contain in their
forms the essence of the plays. Likewise the planetary seals. The forms
of the seals can be a very beneficial study for teachers.[13]

---

[13] Berta Meyer-Jacobs, *The Gem Book – hints and sketches by Rudolf Steiner*, H. Collison,
1932.

This is Heaven speaking to Mother Earth.

Adults today can still experience the will impelling power of form through a very simple experiment. If, for instance, a picture on the wall is crooked, inner effort is made to straighten it. Children live *within* the forms around them. Should a ceiling be low, arched or high, it becomes a vivid dreamlike experience of form to the children. The child must enter and become one with a form in order to withdraw and look at it as a spectator or as an adult from outside. The word-blind or dyslexic child can only withdraw partially.

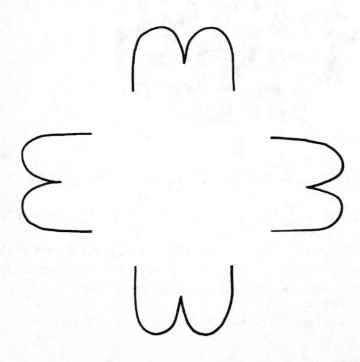

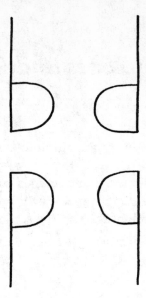

These letters are identical forms to the very young or dyslexic child who is still living in form. The consciousness of the dyslexic child switches from being one with the letter forms to being able to look at them from 'outside' as a spectator.

It is of utmost importance that we practise form movement and form drawing in an imaginative way with the children. Form drawing is not the making of pleasing patterns but an activity which strengthens those forces, the formative life forces the child needs for learning and later for thinking. Form drawing is akin to Eurythmy. Both these subjects were introduced into the Steiner School curriculum as unique and necessary for the healthy development of the modern child.

How can we translate this for the children of classes I and II?

Straight Lines and Curves

Form Drawing

Ribbon patterns often called by the children 'running patterns' can be carried out as follows:

   All the desks or tables are put together to form a long surface. Newsprint or lining paper is clamped down on them. The first child draws a rainbow or the arch of the sky, the second child the bowl of the earth.

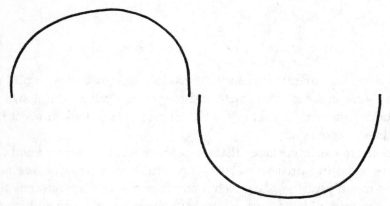

When everyone has finished, the children move around the tables at the same time drawing over their neighbours' arches and curves, trying to make them more beautiful. All along and around the tables they go and when a good wavy pattern appears at the word 'turn', they retrace their steps, drawing arches over the earth and curves under the rainbows and thus a beautiful plait is created.

The children can then move this pattern. Two and two they face each other, giving first right hand, then left, dancing in and out along the waves. This pattern can be built up slowly in movement from Class I to Class IV. The same can be done with zig-zags.

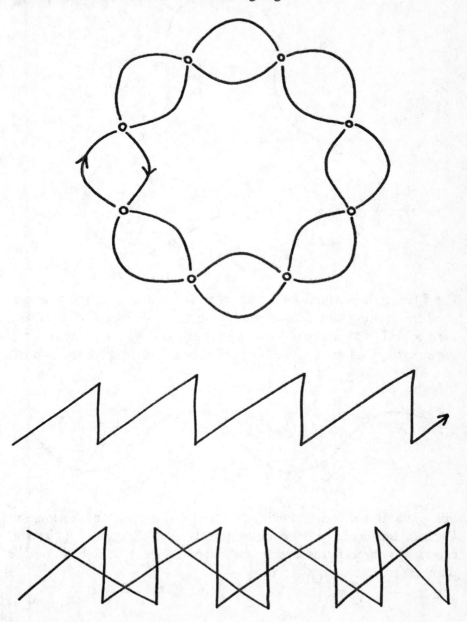

In Class I every other child in the circle can be a tree or a stone while the wind blows around the trees or the stream flows around the stones.

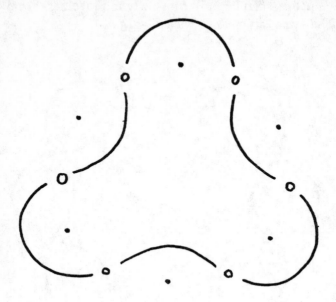

For Class I there could be a pattern story: A prince or the youngest good-for-nothing son follows a winding river, crosses a straight and narrow bridge, a spiral path into and out of a gloomy forest. He sees zig-zag streaks of lightning and finds a starry five pointed jewel and so on.

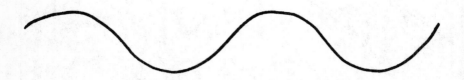

For Class II children a fable such as the Hare and the Tortoise or Uwungalama could be done in movement. The children can follow and experience these forms deeply and then the story bit by bit can be drawn as patterns, not pictures.

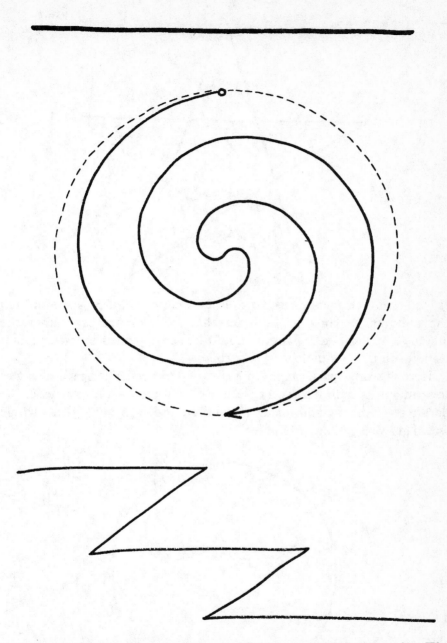

In this way the Maoris, Aborigines and Africans held their stories. The patterns re-awakened the story, the memories and mood in the child's mind.

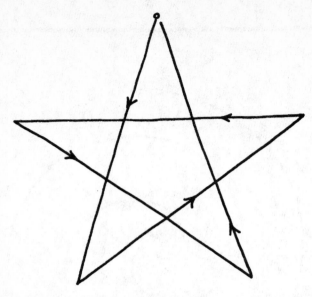

It is not enough for the teacher to draw a pattern on the board and tell the children to copy it. In order that the children experience the language of form each pattern should be accompanied by an imagination, it could be a simple story like this.

Here is a tiny spark caught in a ring of darkness. The spark struggles to send out its light here and here, and here it pierces the darkness. The darkness gives way and makes a cloud around each ray and the whole world grows brighter and lighter.

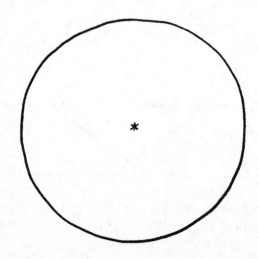

Nora von Baditz[14], one of the first Waldorf School teachers, tells how Rudolf Steiner expressed the need to bring order into chaos especially in Class I. This can be done in the following way. If, for instance, the children tend to be noisy and fidgety let them dance or run around the classroom and at the sound of a drum or a 'magic word' they must all be sitting on their chairs. Or let them dance to music and when the music stops form a ring or a straight line, a half moon or a box (square).

Or play the story of the two wizards:

> *There was an old wizard*
> *Who lived under a stone*
> *And he was grey, so grey*
> *And he made magic for himself alone.*
> *Another wizard lived under the sun*
> *And he made magic especially for Class One.*

This wizard liked to see everyone happy – he liked the people to dance and sing and when he struck his drum and said the magic word Allebezuki bong! wonderful shapes would appear, a silver box (a square). The next time after the dancing and singing and the magic word, a golden ring (a circle), then a spear of light (a diagonal line), a rainbow (an arc), a twinkling star and even a windmill (a cross) or mountain. Later letters can be formed by a group of children or 'run' by one child while the children watching 'read' the letter. At first the letter may be upside-down or sideways-on but the children gradually learn to

[14] Nora van Baditz, 'Ideas and Encouragement for Teaching Eurythmy'.

form it so that it is 'readable' by those watching, thus achieving a withdrawing from living in the form to a spectator or adult consciousness.

Form drawing verse for Classes III, IV or V.

Waves and Ship

I'll sing you a song of the waves of the sea
 Yo-ho, my lads, yo-ho!
I'll sing you a song of the waves of the sea
They're large and wet and cold as can be.
Turn to the left So pull boys, pull for the shore
 When the winds begin to blow.
 When the winds begin to blow.

I'll sing you a song of the Isles of the sea
 Yo-ho, my lads, yo-ho!
I'll sing you a song of the Isles of the sea
With cannibals under a coco-nut tree
Turn to the left So pull boys, pull for the shore
 When the winds begin to blow.
 When the winds begin to blow.

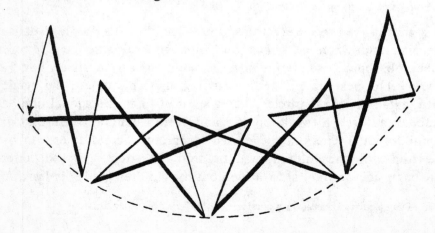

The Tale of the Name of the Tree   An African fable

Play begins with someone playing the bamboo flute and soft drumming.
Actor(s) of the tree are lying on the stage, surrounded by branches.

Narrator:	Long, long ago, my friends, there came a great famine in the land ... and everyone was hungry.
	Now in the land there grew a great tree with fine fruit...

Tree actor(s) stand up slowly, holding branches with fruit.

> But it was known that this fruit would only drop when someone spoke the name of the tree. So as the famine grew worse and worse, the people all came and lived near the tree, waiting for the fruit to ripen.

All the other actors make entrance through rear gate, in a single file, and they are holding bowls in their hands.

> When the fruit was almost ripe, it was found with dismay that no one knew the name of the tree!

Chorus A:	Let us send the swift hare to the Chief over the mountains so that he might tell us the name of the tree.
All:	Speed you well to bring the name
	Hurry, hurry back again!

Flute player plays a tune, hare sets out and comes to the Chief.

Hare:	Greetings, oh Chief! Can you tell me the name of the great tree which stands in our village?
Chief:	The name of that tree is U-wun-ge-lay-ma. When you get back stand beneath the tree, say the name, and the fruit will fall.
Hare:	Thank you Great Chief.
Narrator:	Now the hare was in such a hurry to get back, that he didn't watch where he was running, and he tripped over a root and rolled down a hill.

As hare approaches the village there should be a drum roll which should stop when the hare nears the tree.

Hare: U-wun-ga-tu-ma!
People: U-wun-ga-tu-ma!

Tree shakes its head no

People: Fie, fie, fie for Shame
                   How could you forget the name?

People shake their fingers at the hare and she slinks away feeling ashamed.

Chorus B: Let us send the Giraffe, for he is so swift he will return
                   before he has forgotten the word.

All: Speed you well to bring the name
                   Hurry, hurry back again!

Flute player plays as Giraffe sets out and arrives at the Chief.

Giraffe: Greetings, oh Chief! Can you tell me the name of the
                   great tree which stands in our village?

Chief: That tree is called U-wan-ge-lay-ma.

Giraffe: Thank you Great Chief.

Narrator: The Giraffe set out on his way home, but he stopped to
                   eat some delicious green leaves and before long, the
                   name of the tree had gone out of his head!

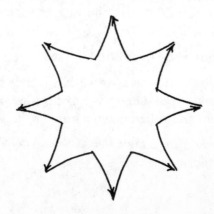

People: Fie, fie, fie for Shame
             How could you forget the name?

People shake their fingers at the Giraffe who feels ashamed and slinks away.

Chorus C: We must send the goat, for he is strong and determined
             and will not stop to nibble leaves.

All: Speed you well to bring the name
             Hurry, hurry back again!

Flute player plays as Goat departs for the Chief.

Goat: Greetings, oh Chief! Can you tell me the name of the
             great tree which stands in our village?

Chief: That tree is called U-wun-ge-lay-ma.

Goat: Thank you Great Chief.

Narrator: The goat hurried back, but he caught his horns in the
             branches of a tree. By the time he was disentangled, he
             could no longer remember the name.

Drum roll as goat approaches tree.

Goat: U-wun-tu-gay-la!

People: U-wun-tu-gay-la!

Tree shakes its head no

People: Fie, fie, fie for Shame
             How could you forget the name?

Chorus D: Now we must send the Lion, for he is both swift and
             strong, and he has no horns to catch in the trees.

All: Speed you well to bring the name
             Hurry, hurry back again!

Flute player plays as lion departs.

Lion: Greetings, oh Chief! Can you tell me the name of the tree
                which stands in our village?

Chief: That tree is called U-wun-ge-lay-ma.

Lion: Thank you Great Chief.

Narrator: As the Lion was on his way home, he became very sleepy
                and he lay down by the side of the road to rest. When he
                awoke, he couldn't quite remember the name of the tree!

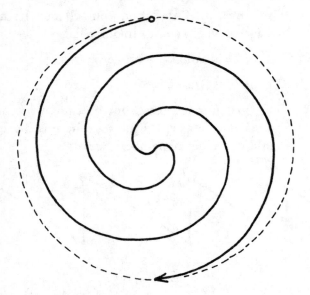

Drum roll as lion approaches the tree.

Lion: The name of the tree is U-way-ma-luna.

People: U-way-ma-luna.

The tree shakes its head no.

People: Fie, fie, fie for shame
                How could you forget the name?
                Friends, let us send brother Tortoise.

Everyone laughs.

Lion: Let him go – we have all failed, so let him fail also.

Narrator:	Before the tortoise set off on his journey, he went to his mother.
Tortoise:	Mother, how does one remember a very hard word?
Mother:	My son, if you wish to remember it do not stop saying it for any reason.

People sing as tortoise goes on his journey.

How can we find the name of the tree?
We sent the hare, he slipped on his knee.
Giraffe got hungry, forgot the name;
Goat got caught and came back in shame.
The lion roared and fell asleep.
And tortoise slowly, slowly creeps;
Slowly, surely he makes his way –
Give him a push, he'll be home today.
Give him a push, he'll be home today.

Tortoise:	Greetings, oh Chief! Can you tell me the name of the great tree which stands in our village?
Chief:	The name of the tree is U-wun-ge-lay-ma.
Tortoise:	Can you say that again?
Chief:	U-wun-ge-lay-ma.
Tortoise:	Thank you great Chief!

Tortoise sets off saying the name over and over. When he gets to his house his wife comes out.

Wife:	Dear husband, you must be so tired. Will you not come in and rest?
Tortoise:	U-wun-ge-lay-ma.

Drum roll as tortoise approaches. He stops under the tree.

Tortoise:	U-wun-ge-lay-ma.
People:	U-wun-ge-lay-ma.

The tree smiles and throws down its fruit-laden branches and the people cheer.

All join hands and skip around the tree singing:
> Now we can speak the name of the tree
> We shall no longer hungry be!

Winding through the crowd and the children can join in ...

Dramatised by Christina Inglis

Class III

In the 9th year the child begins to experience himself as separate from his/her family and surroundings. This can be a very lonely time for the child. This experience is expressed in the games children choose to play. Games where one individual is alone against the world or is the odd one out. Games such as *Pig in the Middle, Hide and Seek, Tag, Tick,* or *Touch Wood, Tom Tiddler's Ground,* and *Ferry Man.*

What do the children need in order to be able to come to terms with this new life-situation?

The children need above all a sense of security. How can they gain this sense of security when they feel their perception of the world is changing so radically and they are very much alone? Some lessons suddenly present difficulties for them. Children often begin to doubt whether their parents are really their parents or if they have been adopted. Many uncertainties, previously unknown, creep into their lives.

The curriculum of Class III can give the child the support he needs: the farming, housebuilding and the Old Testament stories.[15] These lessons give the child stability and the feeling that he is not alone in this world.

The child also needs exercises which will bring him an awareness of himself and also a stretching, reaching out into the world and to others. Again one can introduce 'body geography'. 'Put your right little finger on your left big toe'. 'Put your right ear on your right shoulder' and so on. Also 'Simon says: "Do this"'. All the children imitate 'Simon' who makes a movement such as clapping his hands above his head, he continues making different movements accompanied by the words 'Simon says "do this"'. Eventually he says 'do this' without the 'Simon says' and any child doing that movement is 'out'.[16]

---

[15] Caroline von Heydebrand, *The Curriculum of the Waldorf School.* Also Rudolf Steiner's *Curriculum for Waldorf Schools*, Karl Stockmeyer.

[16] As above.

In the ninth year the children no longer need to learn by imitation; now they must begin to work by themselves and know what they are doing and practise. Thus this is the time and *NOT* earlier, to begin concentration or counting exercises.

All games such as *Statues, Grandmother's Footsteps* (America, *Red light, Green light*). *What's the time, Mr. Wolf?* are usually played at this age; if, however, the children no longer know them, they should be introduced. The running is an expansion, the standing a contraction; this experience is a wholesome one for the child at this time.

In the 9th year the imitative forces become to a certain extent transformed into a new relationship with language. It is good to begin speech exercises at this time, especially in Class IV. Classical rhythms can also be introduced now, as stated previously on page 28, Footnote 9.

Rhythmical poems and verses such as *Tubal Cain, I will go with my Father a-ploughing, To Sea, to sea, Speed hence, speed hence* and so on[17] can be practised so that the rhythm carries the child onward. Rhythms should not be stamped into the ground or used like a metronome. They should lend wings to the children's heels and give added expression to the poem.

It should be mentioned that specialist teachers such as language teachers, singing teachers, eurythmists, should use the same themes in their lessons as the class teacher. For example, during the farming period, teach French and German farming songs, English farming songs and farming poems in eurythmy. This experience of all the teachers working together will give the children the sense of security they need at this time in their development.

At this stage, children no longer learn by imitation but by practising.

Songs and verses connected with main-lesson activities: brickmaking, planting wheat, bread and butter making, measuring and weighing games.

Opening Exercise

Breathe in and out
Fresh air we breathe

[17] For other verses in support of the Main Lessons:
E. Gmeyner and J Russell, *The Key of the Kingdom*, Anthroposophical Publishers, and W M von Heider, *Come unto these Yellow Sands*, Steiner Schools Fellowship. *And Then Take Hands*, Celestial Arts, Milbrae, California.

To grow tall and strong
Is what we need.

Bending and stretching
Tall and straight grow the trees
But they bend in the breeze
 And they sway
This way and that way
And down to the ground.

Threshing song
Threshing, threshing, threshing away
Threshing the golden corn all day,
The golden, golden corn
Far on the winds shall the chaff be borne.

You twiddle your thumbs and clap your hands
And then you stamp your feet,
You turn to the left, you turn to the right,
You make your fingers meet.
You make a bridge, you make an arch,
You give another clap,
You wave your hands, you fold your hands
Then lay them in your lap.

Right foot in,
Left foot out,
Clap our hands
And turn about.

Right foot out,
And left foot in,
Clap our hands
And round we spin

Now we go to and fro
To and fro etc.
 STOP
Which foot is inside?

Heads and Shoulders

adapted from a Cornish Folksong

Head and shoulders knees and toes, knees and toes;
head and shoulders knees and toes, knees and toes
and eyes and ears and mouth and nose;
head and shoulders, knees and toes, knees and toes.

Lubin Loo

Chorus
Here we go Lubin Loo,
Here we go Lubin Light,
Here we go Lubin Loo,
All on a Saturday night.

1. Put your right foot in,
   Put your right foot out,
   Shake it a little, a little
   And turn yourself about.

2. Put your left foot in...
3. Put your right hand in...
4. Put your left hand in...
5. Put your big head in...
6. Put your whole selves in...

The children jump into the ring, turn and jump out

Lubin or Looby means leaping
A ring game: all leap or dance around and stand still for the actions

I will go with my father a-ploughing

I will go with my father a-ploughing
To the green field by the sea,
And the rooks and the crows and the seagulls
Will come flocking after me.
I will sing to the patient horses
With the lark in the white of the air,
And my father will sing the plough song
That blesses the cleaving share.

I will go with my father a-sowing
To the red field by the sea,
And the rooks and the gulls and the starlings
Will come flocking after me.
I will sing to the striding sowers
With the finch on the flowering sloe,
And my father will sing the seed song
That only the wise men know.

I will go with my father a-reaping
To the brown field by the sea,
And the geese and the crows and the children
Will come flocking after me.
I will sing to the weary reapers
With the wren in the heat of the sun,
And my father will sing the scythe song
That joys for the harvest done.

Seosamh Maccathmhaoil.

from *Tubal Cain* by Charles Mackay
This should be accompanied by the beat of a drum

Old *Tubal Cain* was a *man* of *might*
  In the *days* when *Earth* was *young*;
By the *fierce* red *light* of his *furnace* bright
  The strokes of his hammer rung; — *drum*
And he lifted high his brawny hand
  On the iron glowing clear,
Till the sparks rushed out in scarlet showers,

As he fashioned the sword and spear. — *drum*
And he say – 'Hurra for my handiwork!
    Hurra for the spear and sword!
Hurra for the hand that shall wield them well,
    For he shall be king and lord! — *drum*

But a sudden change came o'er his heart,
    Ere the setting of the sun,
And Tubal Cain was filled with pain
    For the evil he had done;
He saw that men, with rage and hate,
    Made war upon their kind,
That the land was red with the blood they shed
    In their lust for carnage, blind.
And he said – 'alas! that ever I made,
    Or that skill of mine should plan,
The spear and the sword for men whose joy
    Is to slay their fellow man.'

And for many a day old Tubal Cain
    Sat brooding o'er his woe;
And his hand forbore to smite the ore,
    And his furnace smouldered low.
But he rose at last with a cheerful face,
    And a bright courageous eye,
And bared his strong right arm for work,
    While the quick flames mounted high.
And he say – 'Hurra for my handicraft!'
    And the red sparks lit the air;
'Not alone for the blade was the bright steel made,'
    And he fashioned the first ploughshare.

Class IV

Children between the ages of nine and ten often want to run away to see the world. They haven't realized before that there is an 'outside world'. This longing to see the world is met in the main lesson periods. Home-surroundings, Man and Animal and also the Norse Mythology lead them to begin to discover themselves and the world. The work with grammar brings structure into language and helps to give children stability.

Counting exercises can become more demanding. Memory training should be continued, also form drawing.

In all our teaching we must seek to engage the children fully; this is another way of strengthening the formative cognitive forces.[18] If children are not wholly engaged they grow tired and bored. We teachers must bring real experiences and enthusiasm to the children.

Games are a necessary part of life and learning, they usually grip the children wholly.

Now the children naturally begin to play games in which one child is alone at first and gradually others gather to help him.

Examples: *Fish, fish come into my net*
                 The Hawk and the Chickens
                 Cat and Mouse (with all its variations)
                 Two and Threes
                 Sardines
                 Tug of war
                    (2 begin and others are quickly added)

Other games in which certain skills are practised:
                 Hopscotch
                 Five stones (fives, knuckle bones)
                 Marbles
                 French skipping
                 Double Dutch
                 Memory and Riddle-me-ree games.
                 Stilts

[18] Rudolf Steiner, *Overcoming Nervousness*, page 9.

Rhythm

In the 9th year children begin to awaken to a new relationship with language; this is a moment the teacher must grasp and encourage. If left too late or used too early, much that this special time in children's development brings will be lost. Before the ninth year children should not be made to move according to classical or musical rhythms.[19] It is too early to confine their feet to a strict rhythm. They can march or dance along and enjoy movement. If they keep to the rhythm of music or poetry naturally it is fine, if not, it does not matter before the ninth year.

During the period in Steiner Schools called 'Man and Animal' the children's awareness of rhythm can be evoked. Children still have something of the 'Proteus' nature at this age, and they can slip inside the movements of animals. Ask them to walk around the classroom like cows and they will plod slowly and perhaps lie down, no one will gallop, a galloping cow is unnatural and ridiculous. Out of this slow plodding a verse will arise, a child's effort to describe a cow (not always great poetry).

Cows are sleepy,
Cows are dreamy,
Cows make milk
All white and creamy

The children can become eagles floating on the air currents or plunging down to capture their prey. Here is a small boy's verse written as a riddle:

Skyhigh I hover and fly,
Blue speck, I drop to the depths,
Huge wings
Golden spread.
King, king of the air,
Who am I?

After prancing around the classroom v -, v - as deer.
This was written also as a riddle.

From Rock to rock
We leap, we bound,

[19] Rudolf Steiner, *Art in the light of mystery wisdom*, Lecture 2: 'The Realization of Tone in the Human Being', Rudolf Steiner Press, London.

Our heads held high
With antlers crowned.

The seals are at one with waves but clumsy and awkward on land. This was an 'instant' verse created by the whole class, different children suggesting the various lines.

Swimming and gliding,
turning and diving,
We are at home
Where white horses are riding.
What are we?

It is a risk but a worthwhile one to write class poems and class plays; the children very soon help each other to find the 'right' words. This encourages a love and taste for language and lays the foundation for future writing.

Grammar

Eight or nine year old children need to experience 'structure' in as many ways as possible. Grammar provides structure together with this new relationship to language. Nouns, 'naming words', and verbs, 'doing words', are introduced in Class III in connection with the Bible Stories – Adam names all living things. The verbs tell what all the animals do and how they move.

In Class IV the other parts of speech are introduced; their work in the sentence is brought to the children. For instance, take a simple verse or short story such as:

An old fisherman and his wife lived by the sea. On a cold, windy day the old fisherman rowed far out to fish. He fished and he fished. Suddenly he hooked an enormous fish. 'Oh, help!' he cried, 'my boat is slowly sinking' ....

To begin, let all the children run from one end of the room to the other every time they hear a verb – then place a chair or two and choose children to be the important naming words. These naming words, the nouns, sit and stand up whenever they hear a noun. In the meantime the verbs keep running. Gradually introduce the other parts of speech with their activities in the sentence.

Pronouns are chosen to stand behind the nouns' chairs. They take the place of the nouns. They stand in for the nouns and when they are mentioned they move proudly in front of the seated nouns. *The verbs keep running, the nouns standing.*

The *prepositions* are the sign-posts indicating with gestures in which direction the nouns are to be found: by the sea, and so on. *The verbs keep running, the nouns standing, the pronouns moving in front of the nouns.*

The most popular parts of speech are the conjunctions, 'joining-up-words' and the interjections, 'exclamation words'. For *conjunctions*, two children take their places opposite each other at either side of the room. By each conjunction they run towards each other, clasp hands and run back to their places.

The *interjections* stand on chairs or a bench and 'throw' themselves into the sentence by jumping down.

Adjectives are chosen to stand beside the nouns and describe them by miming. ie. 'old', 'cold', 'windy'.

Adverbs chase after verbs and mime their action – 'far out', 'slowly'.

Once the children understand the work of one part of speech in the sentence a new one can be added until all the children are actively engaged and listening for their parts of speech.

At this age children have a natural fondness for riddles. This 'craze' can be taken up by the class teacher and led into a deeper experience of the noun. The riddle says everything about a person or an object except the name. There are a thousand Anglo-Saxon riddles from which to choose. Most are alliterative. This Nordic verse-form in which consonants sound and resound can be stepped or stamped forward in a wedge formation or round the circle. Rudolf Steiner gives a vivid description of how the people of the North marched into battle and vanquished the Romans.[20] It is good to practise alliterations out of doors on windy days so that the children have to exert themselves and can feel like the Vikings of old battling against the elements. All this can enhance the Norse mythology, from a time when the Name was sacred. Swords and shields had names. No one had power over another, be he man or god, unless his name was known. See the story of Odin and the Wala.

This riddle motif can also be used in Class IV when the children learn about the animal kingdom. They can describe an animal and its habitat in detail and let the class find the name. In Class V also in the Botany Period, plants or trees can be described without mentioning the name. The class then has to guess. This way of working lays the foundation for exact observation which is introduced later in Class VI at the age of 12.

[20] Rudolf Steiner, *Karma Lectures*, Volume I, Lecture IX, 15th March 1924.

Time and Space

This is a ninth year experience which is brought to the children in Steiner Schools in the period called *Home Surroundings*. Here History and Geography are combined in a very simple way. The children are led from their home base out into the environment, the local legends and history as well as the beginning of map reading are taught. The children learn the points of the compass. This gives them a wonderful feeling of security: the knowledge that if they have a compass they can never get lost! Apart from helping the children to write and act a play about a local legend, another activity could be a treasure hunt. The teacher could show the children an 'ancient', charred map marked 'Buried Treasure' with strange signs and numbers, such as NW24, W30 etc. which the children will soon discover means twenty-four steps to the North West then thirty to the West. Every child will be enthusiastic and keen to find the treasure which should be a box with something in it for each child. For instance, some polished pebbles. In planning such an exercise, the teacher must remember that a child's step or stride is smaller than an adults.

It is especially important for children in their ninth or tenth year that they be wholly involved in the learning process, that they warm to their work.[21] This is the time when the word 'boring' easily creeps into their vocabulary. Children are full of vigour and energy and can become destructive and disturbing if they are not fully occupied and enthusiastic about the subject matter in hand.

Memory Training[22]

This should be practised at this time. It can also help to deepen the child's experience of grammar and language. *The adjective* describes the noun in such a way as to pin it down, to define it, to take away our freedom to chose and imagine the noun. For instance: ask the children to think of a tree. The children will probably all think of different trees, the task of the adjective is to specialize and bring the picture of one particular tree. The first child says, for example, 'a tall tree'; the next, 'a tall, leafy tree'; 'a tall, leafy, ancient tree' and so on. Each child adds a new fitting adjective after repeating what has preceded his or her addi-

---

[21] Rudolf Steiner, *Overcoming Nervousness*, ibid.
[22] Rudolf Steiner, *Overcoming Nervousness*, ibid.

tion. (*The teacher will probably find that the last children will have secretly
been writing the sequence on their hands!*)

A similar 'game' can also be played in Class V using adverbial clauses
or phrases: "The storm wind roared round the house". "The storm wind
roared round the house and bent the trees", and so on.

Grammar was once one of the seven liberal arts but today it tends to
become dry and boring. Through movement, physical and mental, we
can bring life into it.

Two Anglo-Saxon riddles:

The Plough

Class IV

My beak is below, I burrow and nose
Under the ground, I go as I'm guided
By my master, the farmer, old foe of the forest.
Bent up and bowed at my back he walks
As he forces me forward over the field.
I gnash at the ground and tear with my teeth
When my master is strong and can steer me with skill.

The Shield

I am a lonely being, scarred by swords,
Wounded by iron, sated with battle-deeds,
Wearied by blades. Often I witness war,
Perilous fight, nor hope for consolation,
That any help may rescue me from strife
Before I perish among fighting men;
But hammered swords, hard edged and grimly sharp,
Batter me, and the handwork of the smith
Bites in the castles; I must ever wait
A contest yet more cruel. I could never
In any habitation find the sort
Of doctor who could heal my wounds with herbs;
But cuts from swords ever increase on me
Through deadly contest, both by day and night.

Volospo   from the Icelandic Edda

In years bygone   did Imir live.
There was no sand,   no sea, no salty wave.
There was no earth,   no upper heaven,
But the gap Ginunga   and grass nowhere.
The sons of Bur   built up the Land,
moulded Mitgard   the matchless earth,
Sun shone southward   on stoney wastes.
Green sward grew   from the ground.
Sun in the south   minded her moon,
held her hand   over heaven's rim.
Sun knew not   what seat she had,
Stars knew not   what stead they held,
Moon knew not   what might he had.
Gods gathered together, Holy hosts held council,
To night and new moon names they gave,
morning also and midday, dusk and dawn
for the telling of time.

Grammar Verse

Nouns are names of things and places.
Adjectives the names describe.
Verbs are doing, moving, telling
Always busy and alive.
Pronouns take the place of nouns
Adverbs work to qualify
Telling more about the action
How and when and where and why.

Prepositions are like servants,
Leading nouns to find their places,
While conjunctions are like bridges
Linking clauses, words and phrases.

Speech Exercises

C

C is cutting, clear and bold,
Crystal and icy, crackling and cold.

B

Blossoms, beautiful and bright
Bursting into bloom,
Bees and butterflies in flight
By the banks of broom.

W

Wifting wafting, wifting wafting
Waves the weeping willow,

R

Round and round the rugged rock
The ragged rascal ran,

D

Down down deep in the ground
Writhes and wreaths the dragon.
High in heaven in shining might
Michael's meteors glimmer bright,

T

Tip toe, tip toe, ratter ta tat, who's there?

F

Fire fairies fly through flame and fire.

G

The great, golden gleaming gate
Guards the gorgeous garden.

K

K is in brick, block
    nick, nock,
    flick, flock,
    and Kathrine, kitten

Jonathan Godber

Bean pods, pea pods, seed pods and poppy pods
Split when they ripen and open with a pop.

Peter Piper picked a peck of pickled pepper,
A peck of pickled pepper Peter Piper picked.
If Peter Piper picked a peck of pickled pepper
Where's the peck of pickled pepper Peter Piper picked?

Around the rugged rocks
The ragged rascal ran.

She had a sieve of sifted thistles,
A sieve of sifted thistles she had
For she was a thistle sifter.

Betty bought some butter.
The butter it was bitter.
Betty bought some better butter
To make the bitter butter better.

Hey diddle dinkety poppety pet,
The Merchants of London they wear scarlet,
Silk at the collar and gold at the hem,
So merrily march the merchant men.

Call your cattle, Cowherd
Call your cattle home,
The cold night is coming
And the cruel cats creep.

Rustle and shiver,
Rustle and shiver
The silvery leaves
Of the aspen quiver
For ever and ever
Beside the river.

Prouder than princes
In purple and pearls
The strutting peacocks
Preen and pose,
They spread their peerless tails and prance
In poised and perfect pageantry.

Wild are the waves
When the west wind blows,
White is the whirling spray.
Wheeling and wailing
The wide winged gulls
Swing and swoop and sway.

Hop-pole, ripe pear, deep peace,
Steep place, leap past, sip punch.

Black coat, sack-cloth, bake cake,
Stack coal, rock cot, crack crock.

Elmfield School

Games for Class IV

Mother Hen and Chicks versus The Hawk

Children (chicks) hook themselves together in a long line behind the mother hen. The hawk tries to tag the last chick. If s/he does, the chick is taken to the hawk's nest. If the protecting mother hen tags the hawk first he becomes a chick and joins the line, and the mother then becomes the new hawk.

Tom Tiddler's Ground

One person is Tom in a marked out area – his garden. The rest of the group jump into his garden singing, 'I'm on Tom Tiddler's ground picking up gold and silver'. If Tom touches one of them they are frozen to the wall of his den. They can be rescued by a touch on the hand by one of their group, but if Tom catches these two they are both permanently frozen. The last one caught becomes the new Tom.

Fish, Fish, Come into my Net

'Fish, Fish, come into my net' says the fisherman standing in the middle of the room, to a line of children who stand across the room (river). Those the fisherman touches join hands with him, making a net.

Only the hands (x) on the ends can catch fish. The last one caught becomes the new fisherman.

Is Anyone At Home?

Children stand in a circle. One person, X, runs around the outside, saying; 'Is anyone at home? Knock, knock, knock!' The last child he 'knocks' must run in the opposite direction around the circle. When they meet they both must stop and shake hands and he says, 'How are you today, Susan?' She replies, 'Very well, I thank you.' He: 'Goodbye, Susan'. She: 'Goodbye John'. They then continue running in their directions to the empty place in the circle. The first one to get there begins the game again.

Hares and Hounds

One person is 'the hound'. When he chases someone a third person can cross between them, compelling the hound to follow him. Variation: hound cannot tag the hare if he is touching another hare OR is touching wood.

Russian Handkerchief

One child goes round the outside of circle and holds a handkerchief between two children, who then run in opposite directions, shake hands when they meet, run on and see who takes the handkerchief first.

Cat and Mouse   Scotland

'Mousie, mousie come out of your housie
I'll give you a wee bit of bacon.'
   'No, not I.'
'Mousie, mousie come out of your housie'
'I'll give you a wee bit of cheese.'
   'No, not I.'
'Mousie, mousie come out of your housie
Or I'll bite off your tail!'

Now the cat, outside, tries to catch the 'mouse' who is inside the ring. The circle tries to help the mouse and hinder the cat.

Now is the time for the Maypole dances. They combine rhythm, timing and coordination, discipline and awareness of others. If a child goes wrong, the ribbons tangle and have to be untangled. The children can see their own mistakes without having them pointed out by the teacher.

Maypole Dances

The Barber's Pole

Music:	Three Meet or Shepherd's Hey
Step:	Skipping
Boys behind boys:	1/2 – circle 0
Girls behind girls:	1/2 – circle X

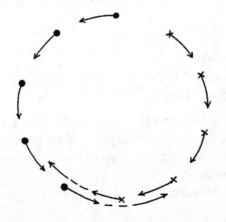

1st round Whole line of boys skip outside circle
  Girls inside
2nd round Whole line of girls skip outside
  Boys inside etc.
Rounds are changed as leaders meet halfway round each time.
Unwind – all turn round to face new leaders at other side of circle.

The Gypsy's Tent

Music: Broom, the Bonny, Bonny Broom or Goddesses
Step: Polka (1,2,3 hop) 2/4 or 4/4 time, a slow graceful step.

Boys stand firm as a rock holding ribbons taut. Girls begin to the
right outside and finish on the right side of the last man. They hand
him their ribbon and take his.
Boys 'undo' the tent.
This is a *slow* dance.

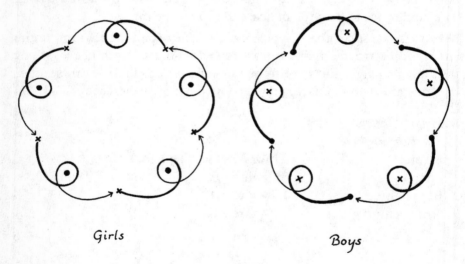

Girls   Boys

The plait or braid

Music: The Rakes of Mallow or Piper's Fancy
Step: Skipping, 2/4 time dance

In Maypole dances the girls always stand on the right of the boys. All
dances *begin* by honouring the Maypole (boys bow – girls curtsey) and
then honouring the partner. All dances *end* by honouring first one's
partner and then the Maypole.
Girls begin in and under.

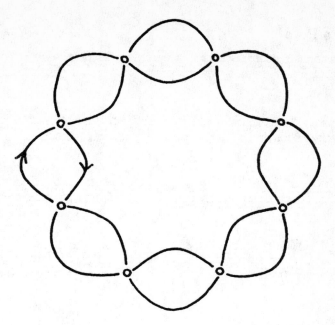

Boys begin out and over.

Always hold the ribbon with both hands so that you can pay it out or pull it in easily.

To unwind – turn and face other direction (corner partner) and undo the plait or braid.

The Gypsy's Tent

Goddesses

Barber's Pole

Three Meet Shepherd's Hey

The Plait

The Piper's Fancy

Class V: Ages 10–11

This is the last year of childhood. The 'Rubicon' of the ninth year with all its waves of insecurities, loneliness, disappointments and apprehensions is past and the children are generally settled and interested in the new subjects for Class V.

The *myths of ancient cultures* are wonderful material for plays also for more advanced work in Grammar. The *study of the plant world and environment* brings new activities. The *geography* of the homeland is a great opportunity for a large scale model of the British Isles. On rainy days when it is not possible to go out to play, newspapers can be torn into shreds and pounded in buckets into thick paste with size. This papier-mâché can be moulded into mountains, river valleys and plains and painted when dry. Pen knives can be sharpened and used to carve light-houses, boats, factories out of balsa wood. Flocks of sheep can be made of pipe cleaners and fleece. Forests of twigs can be planted while the papier-mâché is still pliable. It is not difficult to engender enthusiasm for such a project and have each child happily occupied.

The children now tend to play and work in groups. It is a good time to introduce team games. It often brings an aggressive mood to the games, if the teams are always the same. It is better to pick different groups of children each time the team games are played.

Activities and Games for Class V

Counting Exercise
1 – 4
1 2 3 4 / 1 2 3 4 / 1 2 3 4 / 1 2 3 4
repeat getting faster slowly and slowing down quickly.
Clap-step back on underlined numbers.

The Arjuna Exercise
All children stand in a row and stretch one arm forward and aim at something special, a knot in the woodwork, a crack on the wall, a door handle etc. They must not take their eyes off their goal.

At a given sign they run but at the sound of a drum or cymbals they must stop quite erect without wobbling. The wobblers and those who cannot stop must step out and watch and help spot the last ones to stop.

Twos and Threes
The children stand in a big circle one in front of the other. Two children stand outside the circle, A and B. A chases B. When B stands in front of a couple making three, the child standing at the back becomes B, the one being pursued. If A tags B the pursuing reverses. Those running must not go outside the circle.

Relay and Team Games
Jumping	High jump
	Long jump
Running	Running races
	Relay races
	Rounders

Relay race with a stick (Two or three teams)
The first in the line runs round a post carrying a short stick and gives it to the next child now in front. That child runs round the post and gives the stick to the next in line until all have had a turn. Those who have run go to the back of the line.

Variation:
The stick is taken to the *back* of the line and given to the last child who passes it on; from hand to hand it goes up to the front where the first child takes it and runs round the post.

Ball Over
The two teams in lines – a ball is passed back by throwing it over the head. When the last person catches the ball, s/he runs to the front of the line with the ball and begins again. The team which gets back first to its original position wins.

Ball Under (Through legs)
The same is done only the ball is rolled along the floor through an archway of open legs. Each person can help guide it through.

Race with two sticks
With one long stick in each hand roll a third stick along the floor, across the room, around a post, and back to the next person in line.

Flying Angels
Make a grid for 12 or any even number.
Count 8 steps (or 6) according to space available.
With arms horizontal, the children leap across with 8 (or 6) slipsteps facing their partner to his or her place.
Number ones go first, then number twos and so on.

Variations:
a) When number ones are halfway across (count 4 if 8 steps are the rule). Then number twos begin on the fifth count, and so on.
b) Call pairs at random, for example, *'Fours!* 2, 3, 4, *Sevens!* 2, 3, 4, *Fives!* 2, 3, 4' and so on. Last couple *'Threes!* 2, 3, 4, 5, 6, 7, 8'.

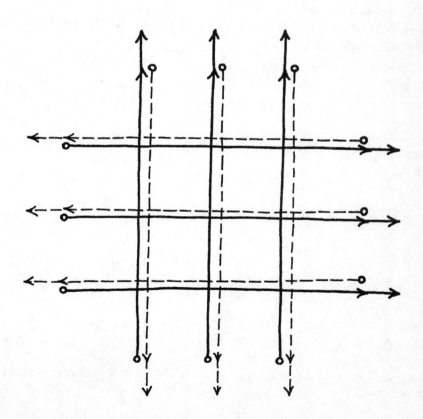

Conclusion

This book is written from one aspect only: the therapy of movement and curriculum associated activities. It is only intended to cover the first ten years of the child's life, the time when a good foundation for healthy learning is necessary.

It is by no means comprehensive. It is, however, meant to point the way ahead and indicate the hurdles and how to contend with them at a time when the learning process is developing. Teachers will recognise this as a working sketch, as guide lines and find their own games and activities to bridge the gaps.

After the eleventh year, the following two years are years of transition from childhood to adolescence. A new age in the life cycle begins with the thirteenth year and the young person makes new demands and has different needs.[23]

[23] Rudolf Steiner, *Meditatively Acquired Knowledge of Man*, Lecture 3, Stuttgart, September 21, 1920.

Bibliography

1. M. Kirchner-Bockholt, *Fundamental Principles of Eurythmy*, Chapter 2, Rudolf Steiner Press, 1977.
   Rudolf Steiner, *Eurythmy as Visible Speech*, Lecture 1, Dornach, 1924.
2. Rudolf Steiner, *Discussions with Teachers*, Volume 1, Stuttgart, 1919–1924; R.S.P., GA 295.
3. Rudolf Steiner, *Discussions with Teachers*, Volume 1, Stuttgart 1919–1924.
4. Rudolf Steiner, *Art as Seen in the Light of Mystery Wisdom*, Lecture 1, December 1914, translation P. Wehrle & J. Collis, Rudolf Steiner Press, GA 275.
5. Rudolf Steiner, *The Gospel of St Mark*, Lecture IV, 1912; R.S.P., GA 139.
6. Rudolf Steiner, *Practical Advice to Teachers*, Lecture 1, Stuttgart 1919; R.S.P., GA 294.
7. Rudolf Steiner, 'Overcoming Nervousness', Munich, 1912.
8. Rudolf Steiner, *A Modern Art of Education*, (Ilkley Course), Lecture II, 1923; R.S.P., GA 307.
9. Nora von Baditz, *Ideas and Encouragement for Teaching Eurythmy*.

An Introduction to and an Appreciation of Earth Education

In recent years there has been a growing awareness of the importance of teaching Rural/Earth Science and Environmental Studies in state schools. Organisations have been founded to support and promote these activities and help adapt the school grounds.[24] Teachers, pupils and parents have transformed many traditional asphalt play areas and boring expanses of mown grass into wild flower meadows, native shrub planting and pond habitats. Here the children can watch the insect and animal life in their everyday surroundings[25] – the wonders of butterflies and spiders, and of tadpoles turning into frogs. They can also have their own gardens if space permits.

Involvement with the environment through these activities, and especially in the form of gardening with the younger children, encourages and nourishes the ability to learn. For example the following qualities can be developed through gardening.

Balance and Skilful Feet and Fingers

Even very young children can gain awareness and respect for plants. They can learn to tread carefully over and between plants. Stepping stones through the garden help to give them joy and dexterity. Their little feet learn to navigate with speed and care. Planting large seeds one at a time, or sprinkling tiny seeds evenly, demands sensitive little fingers.

Rhythm, Anticipation and Movement

The rhythm of the seasons, the daily visit to the garden, going back and forth to the tap with the little watering can, are all special experiences.

---

[24] Landscape Design, 5A West Street, Reigate, Surrey RH2 9BL.
Learning through Landscapes, Eileen Adams, *Journal of the Landscape Institute*, Number 181, June 1989.
[25] *Unlocking the Landscape*, Bill Lucas, *Journal of the Landscape Institute*, Number 221, June 1993.

The eagerness with which children look at the pictures on seed packets and plant seeds and await the first green shoots, the opening of buds and flowers, this is indeed 'enjoying in advance'.[26] However, sometimes a child will dig up bulbs to see if they are growing! Time goes very slowly when one is young and eagerly waiting for something to happen. Patience and restraint are part of the experience.

Creating Order out of Chaos!

It is not always possible in city homes and schools for children to have their own gardens and their gardening has to be limited to beans in saucers and pots on window ledges. This is better than nothing. If, however, children can have their own little garden plot, the first thing they do is to arrange it, place stones around it, then put in plants or seeds and sometimes weeds creating an 'orderly' little garden. This 'orderly' little garden seldom appears orderly or meaningful to the adult but to the child it is his own world which is often arranged and rearranged.

Taste, Touch, Smell and Involvement

Children soon discover how good fresh vegetables taste. Peas in their pods and also baby carrots (sometimes with a smudge of earth on them) taste wonderful! Children can distinguish the smell and feel of herbs and learn their names at a very young age. All these are enthralling experiences which enliven the child's senses. Children are completely absorbed and fully engaged while tending their gardens. Gardening will give children gifts and skills for life.

Although this book is intended primarily to help parents and teachers recognise learning aids for young children aged 3–11, it was deemed necessary to indicate the gardening curriculum up to age 16. It cannot be stressed often enough how essential it is to do the appropriate activity at the right time in a child's development. Teenagers will not benefit from balancing round the garden on stepping stones. Five year olds cannot carry a three year rotation system in their imagination. It is therefore important for a teacher to be aware of what will follow in later years by looking forward and teaching within the context of the whole.

The following gardening program is based on a treatise by Hugh Peters who has kindly allowed his paper 'Gardening with Children' to

[26]   see notes on Classroom gardening.

be included in *Looking Forward*. Hugh Peters, now a class teacher and woodwork teacher in a Canadian Rudolf Steiner school, writes out of his many years of experience, not only of teaching children but also out of a professional background in farming, gardening and environmental work. His concern for the quality of food and nutrition, so important for developing will forces in later life (refer to quote[27]), made him increasingly aware of the lack of appreciation of how plants are grown. The foundation for this appreciation can be laid at an early age but he found little teaching material available for the younger child. His paper makes a very valuable contribution to this area and to the aim of this book.

[27] Dr. Steiner replied when asked why people did not have the will to carry out spiritual impulses:
'This is a problem of nutrition. Nutrition as it is today does not supply the strength necessary for manifesting the spirit in physical life. A bridge can no longer be built from thinking to will and action. Food plants no longer contain the forces people need for this.'

Useful Books for Teachers

Iona and Peter Opie, *The Singing Game*, Oxford University Press.

The Clarendon Books of Singing Games (I and II), Oxford University Press.

Heather Thomas, *Journey through Time in Verse and Rhyme*, Poems collected for teachers of children, Rudolf Steiner Press.

Fellowship Community, *Finger Plays*, Spring Valley, New York, USA.

My Little Puffin, Puffin Books.

Michaela Strauss, *Understanding Children's Drawings*, Rudolf Steiner Press.

Herman Koepke, *Encountering the Self. Transformation and Destiny in the Ninth Year*, Anthroposophical Press, Spring Valley, NY.

Audrey McAllen, *The Extra Lesson*, Robinswood Press, Stourbridge, UK.

Mary Nash-Wortham and Jean Hunt, *Take Time*, Robinswood Press, Stourbridge.

Hans R. Niederhauser and Margaret Frohlich, *Form Drawing*, Mercury Press, Spring Valley, NY.

Rudolf Kutzli, *Creative Form Drawing*, Volumes I, II & III, Hawthorn Press, Stroud, Glos.

Roy Wilkinson, *Common Sense Schooling*, Robinswood Press, Stourbridge.

Roy Wilkinson, *Teaching English* (and other Educational Guides), Rudolf Steiner College Press, Sacramento, California.

W. M. von Heider, *Come unto these Yellow Sands*, Steiner Schools Fellowship, Forest Row, East Sussex, U.K.

W. M. von Heider, *And then take hands*, Celestial Arts, California.

Ann Druitt and Christine Fynes-Clinton, *All Year Round*, Hawthorn Press, Stroud, Glos.

In addition:

Rudolf Steiner's Educational Works (various publishers).

These books are mostly available from:
Rudolf Steiner Press, c/o Biblios, Star Road, Partridge Green, Horsham, West Sussex, RH13 8LD, England.
Tel: 04037 10971

Or from:
Botton Bookshop, Botton Village, Danby, Whitby, North Yorkshire, YO21 2NJ, England.
Tel. 0287 660888

Gardening With Young Children

Kindergarten to Class VI

Ages 3 – 11

GARDENING AS A SPECIALIST SUBJECT

Ages 12 – 16

Revised 1994

Hugh Peters

Prologue

When I undertook this independent study, I was conscious from my own experience and from teachers with whom I have spoken that:

a) Gardening, and specifically organic gardening, is not sufficiently dealt with in most schools, although a few have a farm associated with the school, or close by, which the children may visit occasionally.

b) Although many teachers have perhaps a concept of what Bio-dynamic Agriculture is, most have not had the practical experience of bringing these ideas down to earth, certainly not in the way they constantly bring other ideas of Steiner into everyday teaching practice.

c) From my experience in Biodynamic Farming and Gardening and the constant competition with chemical agriculture, it became obvious that there was a lack of awareness as to the very meaning of quality. Therefore I resolved within myself to find a way to help schools, teachers and parents become aware of the necessity for children to learn reverence and appreciation of gardening and farming in the lower classes in the hopes that this would bring more awareness of what constitutes quality.

I wish to give grateful thanks and acknowledgement to these people who have helped by sharing experience I have not yet had:

Olaf Lampson, Vancouver Waldorf School
Molly von Heider, Emerson College, England
Janet McGavin, Waldorf Institute, Detroit

Gardening with Young Children
Kindergarten to Class VI

One does not normally think of a kindergarten teacher or a class teacher teaching gardening as part of the Main Lesson. That usually begins with the farming period in Class 3, in which farming is considered in terms of an ideal farm, a complete organism. At that time the children visit the nearby farms, and hopefully are able to experience something of the normal work of the farm. Then from Class VI on the children will have a garden, perhaps with a person capable of teaching gardening to them.

But most of the work on the attitudes of the children has already been done in the classes leading up to where gardening finds its place in the curriculum. Many of the stories the children will hear, many of the games they will play, the songs they sing, the words they learn, come from gardening and farming. It is upon these and their relationship directly with nature and nature walks, that the children will form their relationship with one of the most important parts of their life.

Most children will not become farmers, many will not become gardeners or even have gardens, but every speck of food they put into their mouths has some relationship to farming. Every beverage they drink, the air they breathe, the water that flows in the rivers has a direct relationship to farming.

As a part of man's involvement with the natural environment the will with which people are able to approach spiritual tasks is also based on this most fundamental of functions. Dr. Steiner replied when asked why people did not have the will to carry out spiritual impulses:

> "This is a problem of nutrition. Nutrition as it is today does not supply the strength necessary for manifesting the spirit in physical life. A bridge can no longer be built from thinking to will and action. Food plants no longer contain the forces people need for this."[1]

For the cultivation of understanding, in their classes the teachers must be conscious of what they are doing. They may do the same work with the children, perhaps even in the same way, but if they are conscious of the import of the work they will be able to help the children with their attitudes and give them one more gift to help them in their evolving being.

The other important point in having gardening as a part of the Main Lesson in all the school years, is the grounding it gives in rhythms. A child, a person, is at home in the great natural rhythm. His body is a part of the rhythm and his soul feels comfortable there. Yet our civilization has spent a great deal of its energy in trying to emancipate us from the 'confines' of these rhythms so that now we are scarcely aware of them. The child is adrift in a world unconscious of rhythms and he is tumbled and tossed by them in a way he doesn't know.

The child must be led to his home in these rhythms, he must be brought into harmony with them so that their strength will help him grow. Gardening does just that. The plants in the classroom impose themselves with their need for the rhythm of watering. Even in such an artificial environment other rhythms will be seen. Children will begin to realize that the plant does not grow much in the winter, but in February and March begins to send out new growth. They will see when the plant wants to flower and when it is having its rest time. They will see how insects come to visit, bees and butterflies, and become a part of the plant for the moment that they rest. They may even begin to notice those other parts of the plants, the little bugs that crawl and eat the plant.

Up until the age of five, the children have no separate relationship with nature in the way they have instant relationships with a ball, water or other people. Of course that would depend a great deal on what the child has brought with him, or what his parents and peers have imparted to him, but in a general way it would be a time to start thinking of the child preparing to meet the natural world. Before then, the flower is to the child a thing, just as a ball or a pillow is. After five, though, children begin to sense the wonder of the living element in the world about them. They begin to notice that a flower has suddenly opened or that ground which was bare a little while before has suddenly grown green.

From five to seven, the children are filled with wonder at all that they see, and they want to imitate. They want to imitate the things their parents and teachers do, particularly those archetypal movements involved in baking, the stirring and kneading, even the grinding of the grain. In the garden they will imitate digging, raking, watering, planting, and sowing seeds. The reverence with which the teacher does this will become part of the children's preparation.

As they live in the age of fairy tales, stories of the beings of sun, rain, snow, wind, how they speak to each other and everything they teach, is very important. There are many stories of the relationships of plants, animals, bees, butterflies, worms, trees – too many to be mentioned. Of these, the best are the ones that are almost like fairy tales, like the story of *How Butterflies Came* by Hans Christian Anderson:

> One day the flowers begged the fairies to let them leave their stalks and fly away into the air.
>
> 'We have to sit here in the same place from morning till night, fairies! Do let us go!'
>
> 'Go then, dear flowers,' said the fairies. 'But you must promise that you will return to your stalks before the sun goes down.'
>
> 'We promise,' called out the flowers as they flew away, red, yellow, and white, over the grass, out of the garden to the great wide meadow beyond. The fairies' garden seemed, suddenly to have taken wings.
>
> As the sun began to set the flowers flew quietly back to their stalks, and when the fairies came, they found each flower again in its place.
>
> 'Well done, well done!' exclaimed the fairies. 'Tomorrow you may fly away again to the meadows.'
>
> As the sun rose the next morning there was a flutter of red and yellow and white as, from every stalk, a pair of coloured wings rose and flapped, then took flight once more over the meadows and fields. And by and by a day came when the petals of the flowers became wings – *real* wings, for the flowers themselves had become beautiful butterflies – red, yellow and white.[2]

Another excellent example of such a story can be found in *The Emerald Story Book* (reference below), entitled *The Story of a Little Grain of Wheat*, by May Byron.[3]

What the teacher gives the child to imitate in these first years of education will become a great part of his future learning. If on the walks through parks, woodland and meadow, or even wasteland or neglected hedgerows, the teacher shows reverence and respect for those plants and creatures he meets, the children will be sure to imitate that reverence. How the teacher receives the gifts which nature has to offer – the taste, the smell, the feel of the berries, nuts and wild fruits, the flowers picked or left, the bright autumn leaves and little insects, butterflies and bugs – will become part of the soul with which the children begin work in the garden in Class 6, when they are 11, and later in adult life.

In Class II (ages 7–8) the fairy tales gradually give way to animal stories, fables, stories of Saints, as the children in their own souls become aware of the souls of animals around them. They begin to respect and have compassion for the animals with which they come in contact. The children see man in a very special relationship with nature, with the world and with God. In the stories of the Saints, and in the stories of some of the North American Indians, they see man gaining inspiration from God, and help from the beasts. In this year it is good for the children to have animal stories of the beasts which help them in their relationship with the earth – the horse and the ox, the cow, sheep, goat, and pig, the sheepdog and police dog, the eye dog, also the dolphins and porpoise which help the fisherman, the 'farmer of the sea'.

The children will want to be where the work is being done. They may want to try digging for themselves, but everything should be a joy for them to experience. Some classes are lucky to have a small plot of a garden which the class can prepare and grow, sowing grass, flowers, cress, bulbs, lettuce and radishes. It will be best to plant those things which grow quickly and may be harvested in the same season, plants that have scent, taste, colour or can be eaten. Some plants and seeds can even be grown in the classroom.

Some form of animal life as part of the class experience could sometimes be helpful. One class could have a fish tank, one a worm box (where the children have to be especially quiet in order to see the worms), another could have a rabbit in a courtyard where it could live almost wild, and the children could draw pictures of it eating and sleeping and write stories about it.

In Class III (ages 8–9) a change comes which is typified by these poems:

Timber

With oak, the old-time ships were laid,
The round-back chairs of ash were made.
Of birch the brooms to sweep the floor,

The furniture was sycamore.
Clogs were of alder, bows of yew,
And fishing rods of bright bamboo.
Willow was used for cricket bats,
And ash again for tubs and vats.
Of pine, the roof beams and the floor
Or for the window frames and door.
Elm made a wagon or a cart,
And maple was for carver's art.
Beech was for bowls, pipes were of briar.
Many a wood would make a fire.
But in the cottage or the hall,
Ash made the brightest fire of all.[4]

What do we plant

What do we plant, when we plant the tree?
We plant the ship which will cross the sea.
We plant the mast to carry the sails;
We plant the planks to withstand the gales –
The keel, the keelson, the beam, the knee;
We plant the ship when we plant the tree.

What do we plant when we plant the tree?
We plant the houses for you and me.
We plant the rafters, the shingles, the floors,
We plant the studding, the laths, the doors,
The beams and siding, all parts that be;
We plant the house when we plant the tree.

What do we plant when we plant the tree?
A thousand things that we daily see,
We plant the spire that out-towers the crag,
We plant the staff for our country's flag,
We plant the shade from the hot sun free;
We plant all these when we plant the tree.[5]   Henry Abbey

Until this time the children have felt themselves a part of everything
that was going on. Imitation was so strong that it was the basis for most
of what the child did and how he related to the world. Now, with the
ninth year, children begin to separate and to question what is around
them. They become insecure. They want their own things and their

own secrets. They doubt their parents, the roof over their heads and the ground they walk on. Steiner Schools have tried to work with this by giving pictures. The cosmic picture of the God of the Old Testament helps the child feel secure about his origins. The period of house building and farming help to bring order into the world about the child. One well-known Steiner School teacher has said this about the farming period:

> The farm is a community of life; it includes the creatures, the plants, the soil itself; it relates to the great cycle of the seasons and leads the gaze from earth to heaven and back again; it comprises so many human activities, in the field, in the barn, at the mill – so many forms of service in which man is seen at his best, as the simple servant and representative of God – the Master who serves the good of all; it reveals man as a being who is *more* than nature and yet who stands fully within nature – one who can *order* life for mutual benefit and blessing – a husbandman.[6]

The farming period is often taken as a study of an 'ideal' farm, that is, in the classroom; but much closer to the ideal would be for the children to go to the farm and see and experience the activities there. For them to muck out the barn and change the bedding of the animals, feed the calves and cats, and to walk in the furrows behind the plough. Steiner stressed the importance of the child knowing the grains and crops the farmer plants:

> Although it may seem absurd, it must be stated that a person who has not learned to distinguish an ear of rye from an ear of wheat is no complete human being. It can even be said that a person who has learned to distinguish between rye and wheat without having observed them growing in the fields has not attained the ideal.[7]

He should learn that what is referred to as weeds in the garden can be beneficial when they are in parkland, field, and hedgerows. It is important that the child does not see dandelions, clover, stinging nettle and dock just as weeds to be pulled and thrown away. When found in the garden these plants should be prized as food for insects or harvested for the benefits they will return to the soil through the making of compost.

Since gardening spans all the seasons, it must be accommodated throughout the school year. Some schools have split it into three parts:

they have an ongoing garden with the autumn and spring preparations; or each child has a little plot and can plant grain, vegetables or flowers and thus experience the autumn and spring preparation and harvest what has been ripening in the summer sun, maybe at the beginning of Class IV. In the autumn the children could visit a farm for the harvest, and again in the spring to get to know the animals.

The Gardening lesson will continue into Class IV. Some teachers have found that the children do not go to the garden as willingly as in previous years. It is rather like a bridge, because in Class IV the children start to study animals and their relationship with man in a way they have not done before. Not only is the farm looked at as a whole, but everything is followed and traced back to its origins. Grain is harvested and thrashed, then ground in a mill and baked into bread. Relationships – man and the animals, cows, plants and earthworms – are enlarged upon – in earlier years they were just indicated in passing. The children come to see how wasps make paper, the queen laying the paper down layer upon layer; how honey bees make wax out of honey and how they gather the nectar and fertilize the flowers at the same time; they learn about the beavers and how they fell trees to make dams. They see how the dams influence the water table for miles around, how the beavers act as stewards of the water ecology. Each animal can do one thing wonderfully well, but man is free to choose what he wants to do. In this way the children come to feel themselves citizens of the earth.

At the very beginning of Geography, the study of Home Surroundings, the children draw maps of the school grounds and the farm they visited. In Class V they look further afield to see where the various gifts of the earth are found and worked with and exported.[8]

Children work intensively with botany, learning about the relationship of the plant with the earth and the sun. They also learn about some of the botanical families. For instance, that many flowers and fruits belong to the roses (apples, cherries, plums, blackberries, etc.) Many have their flowers in a basket (compositae), and many are like butterflies (leguminacae). From their main lesson topics they learn that some plants are gifts from Zarathustra, some have come from Greece and Egypt. They continue to prepare the soil and plant seeds. This practising in the garden is filled with images from their main lessons.

Class V Botany

Behold the plant,
It is a butterfly
Bound to the earth.

Behold the butterfly,
It is a plant
Freed by the heavens.

Rudolf Steiner

From 'To the Small Celandine' Part III

There is a flower, the lesser Celandine,
That shrinks, like many more, from cold and rain;
And, the first moment that the sun may shine,
Bright as the sun himself, 'tis out again!

William Wordsworth

Gardening, Earth Science, as a Specialist Subject

From Class VI upwards, the activities that have been called Gardening take on a new dimension. They become an independent study, taught where possible by a specialist teacher. They can be called Natural/Rural Science or Environmental Studies, or Earth Science and should embrace both practical craft and traditional skills and methodical scientific work.

Up to the age of 12 the children have learnt wonder, reverence, respect, a feeling for living things. They have learnt by imitation and through rhythms and stories and how things were done in the past. Now in Class VI they start looking forward consciously to understand and trace the interrelationships at work in nature and the environment, cause and effect, and to see that their actions can change what happens in the world around them, starting with a little plot of ground. They experience how much effort is required to produce a harvest. Rudolf Steiner stressed how important it is now that the actual gardening be approached seriously as work. The children should feel the pride of a job well done and the shame of a job ill done.[9] Young people need a challenge and the tasks like double digging and composting are physical tasks that give ample reward.

A preparation for geology is begun in Class VI, 'Different soil structures are examined in a simple way to show how different plants require different environments'.[10] They learn how:

> "The Rock rules all things upon its surface. The grasses, the flowers, the trees, the crops, the flocks and the herds, cottages and castles, streams and rivers. Only man is free to wander from rock to rock, to look, learn and receive what strength each one is offering."[11]

In Classes VI, VII and VIII the children learn to draw maps of the school grounds and make plans for the garden area. They work together as a class, no longer each with an individual plot, they lay out a vegetable garden on a three year rotation system. They learn and practise methods of cultivation, planting, composting, fertilizing, harvesting and animal husbandry, and the use of the produce in juice making, drying etc. Rudolf Steiner suggested how the child should learn to pull a small plough, turning the soil with it, begin to use a sickle to cut grass, to mow with a small scythe. A child who has done these things will be a different person from one who has not.[12] In these years the children also begin crafts, they learn to make and use tools. Rudolf Steiner stressed the relationship between gardening and handcrafts. The children also begin the sciences at this age; they learn accurate observation. Here, too, is a relationship with the garden and the farm. What a ladybird larva looks like and does, the life cycle of a butterfly (cabbage white or otherwise), the differences between a centipede and a millipede not only under a magnifying glass but in their activities, the insect and animal life of pond, hedgerow and a spadeful of earth, Ecology and Climate, should all be part of the program. It is no more than is required by the (English) National Curriculum in state schools.

It is however, very important in Classes VI, VII and VIII that the teaching by the specialist should be done in close co-operation with the Class Teacher.

The study of the Roman and Medieval civilizations gives an ideal chance to describe the herb and vegetable gardens of those times. The Age of Discovery and Exploration includes climatic conditions and descriptions of the flora and fauna in newly found lands. This is but one example of how the gardening program can become an integral part of the Class Teacher's work.

In Classes IX and X all that has been done so far is taken a step further. The simple map of the school grounds becomes an accurate survey prepared with the use of surveying equipment and produced as a technical drawing. The young people learn construction, irrigation and forestry. They learn not only how to plant but also to prune and propagate. They are introduced to the theory of plant breeding and genetics (ref. curriculum)*. Though it may not be possible for all these subjects to be taken by one teacher, it is important that the children experience what they are learning as an integrated whole. Dr Pfeiffer writes:

The first essential thing is to awaken in them (the children) a feeling for the forces of growth, for the eternally creative forces of Nature.

* Pages 120 and 121.

The next step is to awaken in them a sense of responsibility toward those forces of growth, towards the health of the soul, of plants, of animals and of men, and also an inner sense of satisfaction in progressing towards this goal ... Those who cannot develop these ethical qualities will never become good farmers or colonizers and they will hardly ever become constructive members of the social organisation.[13]

There is a great deal of work yet to be done in the training of teachers for this important subject. One can no longer assume an adult has experience of or even a relationship to gardening. Even if a teacher does, it requires a strong effort of will to carry this experience into the living pictures one presents to the children.

This short exposition gives but a brief description of the scope of learning felt necessary, not to create farmers and gardeners but to help the children become whole citizens of our civilization.

References

1. Rudolf Steiner, *Agriculture*: Tr. George Adams, Biodynamic Agriculture Assn, London, 1972. (Pref. by Dr. Pfeiffer, p.7).
2. Andrew Lang (Editor), *The Emerald Story Book*, Longmans, London.
3. These stories are especially good in that they say how things are in nature, yet say it in a picture which is exactly suited to 6 or 7 year old children. (There are many other stories in *The Emerald Story Book* and in the *Seven Year Wonder Book* which are most apt.)
4. W.M. von Heider, *And Then Take Hands*, Celestial Arts, California, 1981, p.31.
5. W.M von Heider, *And Then Take Hands*, Celestial Arts, California, 1981, p.31.
6. H. Moore, *Rudolf Steiner's Contributions to the History and Practice of Agricultural Education*, Biodynamic Farming and Gardening Association, P. O. Box 550, Kimberton, PA, USA.
7. Rudolf Steiner, *Practical Advice to Teachers*, Rudolf Steiner Press: London, 1976, Chapter 2.
8. E.A. Karl Stockmeyer, *Rudolf Steiner's Curriculum for Waldorf Schools*, Steiner Schools Fellowship Publications, Forest Row, UK, 2nd Edition, 1965, p.114.
9. Rudolf Steiner, *Conferences for Teachers*.
10. H. Moore, *Rudolf Steiner's Contribution to the History and Practice of Agricultural Education*, Biodynamic Farming and Gardening Association Inc., P. O. Box 550, Kimberton, PA.
11. H. Moore, ibid.
12. Rudolf Steiner, *Practical Advice to Teachers*, Rudolf Steiner Press, London, 1976, Chapter 2.
13. E.E. Pfeiffer, *Soil Fertility, Renewal and Preservation*, London, Faber and Faber, 1949.

Classroom Hints

Care

It is very important how things are done with children. What is stated should be carried through consequently to its conclusion. For example, it is fun to plant things but sometimes they die. Then the dead plants should be disposed of with the same care and attention with which they were planted. Not left to gather dust and disappear, or greet the children dead at the start of a new term. If the children are asked to bring seeds, do not throw into the bin any that are left over – seeds are potentially living plants. The compost heap is a wonderful way of 'giving things back to Mother Earth' with reverence and respect.

In the artificial environment of a classroom, once a seed is planted, it needs to be tended throughout its life. There is a commitment. A child's enthusiasm and anticipation can too easily be turned into disillusionment and disrespect if this commitment is not honoured by the teacher.

Conditions

All plants need different conditions to grow well. A cold north window sill will be ideal for some but others will languish. So choose carefully to suit the facilities available. Generally, flowering plants like more light, leafy plants and ferns more shade. Direct sunlight is damaging to most seedlings, though not enough light will make them weak and spindly. There are exceptions to every rule! Read the seed packet or look up in a gardening book, think how similar plants grow in nature. Include the children in this discovering, they can enjoy finding out and will develop a better understanding than if the teacher does it all and dictates.

Plants not only need different situations to thrive but also varying soil types – gritty, soft and peaty or loamy, acid or limey. The average garden soil without additions is rarely suitable for indoor conditions because of its structure, and it can sometimes bring unwanted pests and diseases. Proprietary mixes can be bought, perhaps advisable for seedlings, but the teacher and children can also make a mixture themselves. The main ingredients are compost, sand/grit leaf mould or peat substitute and loam (which is well rotted turf) and good garden soil. Feel and smell these ingredients individually, sieve and mix them like a cake – it is the plants' food. Make sure everything is clean: flower pots (preferably clay), tools and containers. Old gardening encyclopedias are useful sources of information, ones that predate convenience prepacked potting soils. It is not considered environmentally desirable to use peat any longer; there are substitutes and leaf mould. Charcoal and organic fertilizer are a useful addition.

Feed the plant, also when it is growing. It can not gather all that it needs confined in a pot indoors. Seaweed based fertilizers are considered good, and water carefully from the bottom with water at room temperature. Beware of over-watering and over-feeding, both can kill. Bought pot plants are often grown in artificial, forcing conditions and often die back and get diseased. For a child it is more interesting and enjoyable to start from the beginning.

Seeds
  Mustard and cress, mung beans
    on blotting paper or soil (these are edible seedlings)
  Dill, chervil, lettuce, wheat
    (cut with scissors, eat as green shoots)
  Sweet peas, runner and broad beans
    in earth or against the side of a jam jar lined with blotting paper
    and 1/4 full of water, with the seed above water level, roots and
    shoot can be observed
  Nasturtiums
    in soil, and kept cool and light (edible)
  Marrows and cucumbers
    will flower but may not fruit, unless bees are around. Seeds can be
    saved from them if ripe. Then grow in a warm, light place.

Trees
  Apple pips, peach stones (over winter outside). Fresh acorns, conkers,
  lemon/orange pips, avocado stones.
    Pot on or plant outside when too big (except avocados and citrus).

Bulbs

The hyacinth is one of the most exciting for children to watch if grown in a jar of water with the base almost touching the water, and the shoot covered until well advanced. An onion can be grown the same way or in soil and the leaves eaten.

Autumn crocus, with or without soil (but poisonous)

Plants

Mint, sorrel (wild or cultivated) chives, parsley, rosemary, lavender can be grown as pot plants (best not from seed). Parents may donate cuttings or plants.

Vegetable tops

Carrot, beetroot, parsnip can be grown on saucers for the leaves. The leaves of these are not often seen by children and are quite decorative. Cut the top off a carrot, with ½ inch of carrot, and place in a saucer with a little water – the young leaves can be eaten. A pineapple top will also grow but needs soil and is best left for a few days for the flesh to dry before planting to the depth of the flesh (in warm, light conditions).

Indoor miniature gardens on a plate (with blotting paper or soil)

Children with their small fingers can make some delightful arrangements. Different types can be chosen. For example: 'edible' gardens with carrot or beetroot tops, mustard and cress, small onions— etc. Shady gardens with mosses, liver worts, ivy, small fungi. Lawn gardens with daisies, plantains, buttercups, a pinch of grass seed, any small shallow rooting plant. (Dandelions have deep tap roots). Stone gardens with saxifrage, lichens, stonecrop, house leeks etc. pieces of wood, pebbles. Shells and a mirror for 'water' can be part of the arrangement. Look what is growing outside on old stone walls, gravel and in the lawn.

Spray the gardens with a fine spray of water to keep them damp, especially the mosses.

Animals and Insects in the Classroom
Worms

A worm box is an interesting experience suitable for Class IV. It is a simple wooden box in the corner of the classroom filled with a mixture of soil and leaf mould and covered with boards or black plastic. The soil mixture should be partially composed of composted leaves. Red Wriggler worms are the best variety if they are obtainable from a compost heap or gardening magazine advertisement. Old leaves or grass are put in and the box is tightly covered over. The class can see in how short a time the worms transform leaves and grass into compost. This compost of worm castings is one of the best foods for plants in the classroom. Another benefit is that the children must be very quiet in order to see the worms. It is an excellent demonstration of composting, takes little work, and gives wonderful fertilizer in return. If there are any smells other than a clean, earthy smell, then something is not right, usually too much water or lack of air. Another way to observe the activities of worms can be demonstrated by filling a large jam jar with alternating layers of sand and leaf mould or compost. Include a few worms and place a few old damp leaves, onion shoots or grass on top. The worms will mix the sand and compost surprisingly quickly by their activities.

Caterpillars

Keep dark. Caterpillars can be kept in a glass jar with a muslin or perforated covering and fed on leaves, depending on the type of caterpillar. There should be plenty on cabbages, nettles and privet hedges. (Privet is especially good for stick insects). The caterpillars can be watched until they turn to a chrysalis and the chrysalis kept in the right condition (it varies with the species) until it turns into a butterfly and the butterfly must be let loose.

Snails and slugs

These can be kept the same way and can be quite fascinating to children. It is usually adults that first show disgust. There are many kinds of slugs and snails. There is a lot to a simple snail.

Tadpoles

Are also a favourite with children. But the tadpoles need to be fed with larvae or raw meat and the water kept clean if they are to turn into frogs. It is best to return them to a pond when they start showing legs. The classroom is not a good habitat for a frog.

Be responsible for returning all creatures and insects to the wild and do not leave them to die without food in the hot sun on a window sill in front of the children. Care should also be taken with handling these creatures; frogs, as they are cold blooded, suffer from contact with warm hands.

A magnifying glass and a nature diary will help the children enjoy and appreciate. These are a few suggestions. The children will no doubt have ideas, too, and these can be encouraged. But be sure to check they are feasible.

Seeds for sowing outdoors

Mark out areas (before sowing) with shells or pebbles and label carefully.

Large seeds

(for the youngest children). Sunflowers, sweet peas, beans, nasturtiums, pumpkins, marrows.

Flowers

Nigella (love in the mist), candytuft, cornflower, calendula, pansy, forget me not, poppies (Shirley), flax annual (blue and red). (Stems can be platted or woven when flowers are over). Escholzia, Antirrhinum. Convolvulus (annual). Limnanthes (poached egg flower), Rudbeckia, Virginian stock, Linaria (Toadflax).

Vegetables

Radishes, peas, beans, marrows, pumpkins, spinach or chard. Lettuce (Tom Thumb), beetroot, corn salad, cress, potatoes, strawberries, pot on runners (not as seed).

Summary of the Curriculum for Gardening in Germany

Class I 7–8 years	Class II 8–9 years	Class III 9–10 years Farming	Class IV 10–11 years	Class V 11–12 years
	Cultivation of individual plots under guidance of class teacher			
3 years crop rotation, each class receives its own garden				Grafting/ Pruning Plant breeding Soil Science Fruit growing

Class VI 12–13 years	Class VII 13–14 years	Class VIII 14–15 years	Class IX 15–16 years	Class X 16–17 years
Cultivation: through tillage, planting vegetables and fruit learn what care, effort and patience has to go into cultivation before you can harvest.	Continuation of what has been started in Class VI.	Through 3 years of practical work the children have learned the required methods of cultivation which they will understand in Theory in the following year.	Soil types: Principles of planning a vegetable garden. Crop rotation and tillage. Compost making. Annual and winter hardy plants and bushes. Astronomy Meteorology and Climatology.	As for class IX. Making of tools and maintenance. Landscape work. Making paths. Husbandry. Fertilization/ Grass – Hay. Agricultural problems.

Weaving of mats, making brooms, etc. simple construction work.
Look backward and forward on what has been done in practice.

Theory to support the practice of the last 3 years. The practical work of the summer is consolidated in theory in winter.

Books from Hawthorn Press

CHILD'S PLAY 3
GAMES FOR LIFE
FOR CHILDREN AND TEENAGERS
Wil van Haren and Rudolf Kischnick.

Translated by Plym Peters and Tony Langham.

A tried and tested games book consisting of numerous ideas for running races, duels, wrestling matches, activity and ball games of skill and agility. Its clear lay-out, detailed explanations and diagrams and its indexing of games by age suitability and title makes *Child's Play* an invaluable and enjoyable resource book for parents, teachers and play leaders.

October 1994; 215 × 145mm; 128pp paperback; colour cover; ISBN 1 869 890 63 9

MUSIC FOR YOUNG CHILDREN
Rita Jacobs.

Translated by Roland Everett.

Lullabies, nursery rhymes, worksongs and rounds to feed the soul and form a child's early musical memories. Rita Jacobs sensitively discusses the important role of different types of music at certain stages of children's growth and development. The book contains 15 songs with a further 14 appended by the translator who is a parent and former teacher.

186 × 123mm; 104pp paperback; ISBN 1 869 890 28 0

CREATIVE FORM DRAWING 1, 2 & 3
Rudolf Kutzli.

These three workbooks form a successful series which aim to encourage people to explore in detail the ways in which forms are created. The exercises provided give a fascinating insight into the relationship between form and content.

WORKBOOK 1
297 × 210mm; 152pp;
sewn limp bound; fully
illustrated;
ISBN 1 869 890 28 0

WORKBOOK 2
297 × 210mm; 152pp;
sewn limp bound; fully
illustrated;
ISBN 1 869 890 14 0

WORKBOOK 3
297 × 152mm; 152pp;
sewn limp bound; fully
illustrated;
ISBN 1 869 890 32 9

DRAWING & PAINTING IN RUDOLF STEINER SCHOOLS
Margrit Jünemann and Fritz Weitmann.

This comprehensive account of painting and drawing in the Steiner curriculum combines detailed practical advice with clearly defined philosophy on aesthetic education. The book takes readers carefully through each stage of Steiner art teaching, suggesting appropriate exercises and explaining the reasons for the different developments in the curriculum at appropriate stages of pupils' development. This book is not only a vital reference source for all who are involved in teaching in Waldorf schools, but an inspiration to all who are concerned with children's creative development and fulfilment.

170 × 240mm; 220pp approx; hardback; colour cover; colour and black & white illustrations; ISBN 1 869 890 41 8

RUDOLF STEINER ON EDUCATION
A COMPENDIUM
Roy Wilkinson.

Here is an accessible introduction to the educational philosophy of Rudolf Steiner (1861 – 1925), the pioneer of a comprehensive, co-educational form of education for children from kindergarten through to the end of high school. The book gives a thorough survey of Steiner's ideas, delving deeply into educational matters.

Roy Wilkinson has written and lectured widely on Rudolf Steiner education, building on his many years in school teaching.

216 × 138mm; 168pp; ISBN 1 869 890 51 5

THE TWELVE SENSES
Albert Soesman.
Translated by Jakob Cornelis.

The senses nourish our experience and act as windows on the world. But our stimulation may undermine healthy sense experiences. The author provides a lively look at the senses, not merely the normal five senses, but twelve: touch, life, self-movement, balance, smell, taste, vision, temperature, hearing, language, the conceptual and the ego senses. The imaginative approach provides an accessible study guide for teachers, doctors, therapists, counsellors, psychologists and scientists.

210 × 135mm; 176pp; sewn limp bound; ISBN 1 869 890 22 1

UTOPIE
Michael Stott.

A German language text book for classroom use by class seven.

Jan 1995; 216 × 138mm; 120pp; colour cover; illustrated; ISBN 1 869 890 57 4

VOYAGE THROUGH CHILDHOOD INTO THE ADULT WORLD
A GUIDE TO CHILD DEVELOPMENT
Eva A Frommer.

Human beings have a long infancy during which they are dependent upon others for the means of life and growth — such a book on child development is therefore vital. Many of Frommer's ideas in this book derive from her professional observations as a child psychiatrist and include her personal distillations of Rudolf Steiner's teachings. A deep concern for the uniqueness of each individual child permeates this book, while offering practical solutions to the challenges of raising a child at each stage of his or her development.

October 1994; 216 × 138mm; 140pp approx; paperback; colour and black & white photographs; ISBN 1 869 890 59 0

ALL YEAR ROUND
Ann Druitt, Christine Fynes-Clinton, Marÿe Rowling.

Brimming with seasonal stories, activities, crafts, poems and recipes, this book offers an inspirational guide to celebrating festivals throughout the seasons. A sequel to *The Children's Year*, this book arises from the festivals workshops run by the authors at the annual *Lifeways* conference at Emerson College.

"The words are ours, the festivals are yours." This book encourages both adults and children to explore forgotten corners of the educational curriculum and to develop and adapt the various festivals to fit their own family traditions. The enthusiasm and colourful creativity with which this book is written is guaranteed to stimulate interest in the diverse and multiple joys of the seasons.

July 1995; 200 × 250mm; 248pp approx; limpbound; colour cover; fully illustrated; ISBN 1 869 890 47 7

FESTIVALS TOGETHER
A GUIDE TO MULTI-CULTURAL CELEBRATION
Sue Fitzjohn, Minda Weston, Judy Large.

This is a resource guide for celebration, and for observing special days according to traditions based on many cultures. It brings together the experience, sharing and activities of individuals from multi-faith communities all over the world — Buddhist, Christian, Hindu, Jewish, Muslim and Sikh. Its unifying thread is our need for meaning, for continuity and for joy. Written with parents and teachers in mind, it will be of use to every school and family. Richly illustrated, there is a four page insert of seasonal prints by John Gibbs for your wall.

200 × 250mm; 224pp; limp bound; colour cover; fully illustrated;
ISBN 1 869 890 46 9

PARENTING FOR A HEALTHY FUTURE
Dotty T Coplen.

"Nobody ever told me about children", said one bemused parent. Here is a commonsense approach to the challenging art of parenting; an offer of genuine support and guidance to encourage parents to believe in themselves and their children. Dotty Coplen helps parents gain a deeper understanding of parenting children from both a practical and holistic, spiritual perspective. The book posits sensible suggestions and invaluable insights into ways of bypassing the inevitable hurdles of parenting without compromising the enjoyment of the process.

November 1994; 216 × 138mm; limp bound; ISBN 1 869 890 53 1

ORDERS
If you have difficulty ordering from a bookshop, please order direct from:
Hawthorn Press,
Hawthorn House, 1 Lansdown Lane, Stroud GL5 1BJ UK
Telephone: 0453 757040   Fax: 0453 751138